D1627167

I'm on Facebook— Now What???

How to Get Personal, Business, and Professional Value from Facebook

by Jason Alba and Jesse Stay

20660 Stevens Creek Blvd., Suite 210
Cupertino, CA 95014

Trademarks

All terms mentioned in this book that are known to be trademarks or service marks have been appropriately capitalized. Happy About® cannot attest to the accuracy of this information. Use of a term in this book should not be regarded as affecting the validity of any trademark or service mark.

Warning and Disclaimer

Every effort has been made to make this book as complete and as accurate as possible, but no warranty of fitness is implied. The information provided is on an "as is" basis. The authors and the publisher shall have neither liability nor responsibility to any person or entity with respect to any loss or damages arising from the information contained in this book.

Praise for I'm on Facebook—Now What???

"'I'm on Facebook-Now What???' is a thorough-but-usable dive into what a new user of Facebook might want to know. I can see this book being great to hand to a friend or coworker who wants to get involved in social networks, but really isn't sure which next steps to take. Jason and Jesse have created a great guide that will deliver value to new users, and might even teach a more seasoned user a thing or two."
Chris Brogan, Social Media Advisor,
http://chrisbrogan.com

"A great book, a true reference to those who want to understand the networking values and business opportunities of the Facebook platform."
Jeremiah Owyang, Web Strategist,
http://web-strategist.com

"'I'm on Facebook--Now What???' is the definitive guide to optimizing your Facebook results on both a personal and professional level. Savvy authors, Jason and Jesse packed everything you need to know from A-Z into this quick and easy read. Whether you're just getting started, or you want to build an application, or you want to build your business, you need to pick up a copy of this book!"
Mari Smith, Relationship Marketing Specialist,
http://facebookfortunes.com

"I'm on Facebook--Now What???' offers compelling reasons why Facebook should be a part of everyone's social and professional networking strategy. Facebook is not just for social networking and it's not just for kids anymore. Jason Alba and Jesse Stay convinced me that Facebook is a place where you can have it all...forge and nurture business relationships, promote your ideas, and reconnect with friends. Jason and Jesse teach users how to optimize the Facebook community and have a lot of fun while you are there. I'm hooked!!!"
Barbara Safani, President, http://CareerSolvers.com

More Praise for I'm on Facebook—Now What???

"Jason and Jesse hit a home run here. I've been on Facebook for a long time but many of my family and business associates are just signing on now. Every week I get emails and calls asking me what to do with "this Facebook thing" and half the time I don't even have an answer. Jason and Jesse have an answer and I'll fwd people to this book to hopefully save myself 3 hours a week in Facebook tutoring!"
Richie Hecker, Chief BootStrapper,
http://BootStrapper.com

"Jason and Jesse have undoubtedly spelled out how to use Facebook appropriately, a step-by-step guide if you will. I was not a fan of Facebook until I read this book, now I am utilizing all the features and finding out that you really can network yourself and your business on this site. Thank you so much for writing this, it gives us another avenue besides LinkedIn to get our names and companies out there. Another Kudos!"
Louri Russel Boilard MBA, Executive Resume Writer,
http://www.distinctcareer.com

"Jason Alba has done it again. First he was our navigator through LinkedIn, now he's teamed up with Jesse Stay to give us a primer on how to use Facebook personally and professionally. Before you toss up a profile as an afterthought, or dismiss it as a fad and a teenage timewaster, pick up `I'm on Facebook--Now What???' and find out how you and your business can harness the power of social networking."
Diane K. Danielson, CEO, Downtown Women's Club and co-author of The Savvy Gal's Guide to Online Networking (or What Would Jane Austen Do?)

"'I'm on Facebook--Now What???' is a great overview for the Facebook novice. Want to figure out how to leverage the power of social networking? This book is a must read for those that are confused once they get past the registration form."
Nick O'Neill, Owner, Social Interactive,
http://www.allfacebook.com

"Hold on to your yellow highlighters! I thought I could just breeze through 'I'm on Facebook...Now What???' and notate the REALLY important stuff to know. It became apparent very quickly that whole pages were going to be drenched in yellow. So, my advice is to take your time, enjoy the read and pick out key areas you want to implement immediately (save your highlighting for those). You may even want to prioritize your 'to-do' list generated from the convenient Action Items at the end of every chapter. Then, jump in and get started! With all the resources and support provided, it's like Jason and Jesse are holding your hand the whole way."
Susan Guarneri, Career Assessment Goddess,
http://AssessmentGoddess.com

"Bottom Line: as the authors point out, even if Facebook is a bit hyped, there are practical reasons for investing the time and effort to become a part of it. Perhaps for careerists and business people, the single most powerful reason is that it is offers another way to grow your network in an online environment that is feature rich and even a bit hip! With its rich content, well-documented resources, tips, and end-of-chapter Action Items, this is a must-read guide for novices and experienced users alike."
Walter Akana, Life Strategist and Owner,
http://Threshold-Consulting.com

"Jason Alba's book on LinkedIn (I'm on LinkedIn---Now What???) is an excellent resource for anyone (and that should be everyone) using LinkedIn to network. This time around, Jason, with co-author, Jesse Stay have done the same for Facebook users. It's true that Facebook is no longer just for kids, and every professional should be using it, at least for branding and communicating. This book will show you how you can get the most out of it and it's another terrific resource."
Alison Doyle, About.com Guide to Job Searching,
http://Jobsearch.about.com, http://alisondoyle.com

More Praise for I'm on Facebook—Now What???

"Bottom Line: as the authors point out, even if Facebook is a bit hyped, there are practical reasons for investing the time and effort to become a part of it. Perhaps for careerists and business people, the single most powerful reason is that it is offers another way to grow your network in an online environment that is feature rich and even a bit hip! With its rich content, well-documented resources, tips, and end-of-chapter Action Items, this is a must-read guide for novices and experienced users alike."
Walter Akana, Life Strategist and Owner,
http://Threshold-Consulting.com

"Don't buy this book if you think the internet is just a fad and will be going away sometime soon! Facebook is a great example of how the internet is destined to change many business systems we take for granted today. Do you want to know how this incredible platform can help you in your life, business and career? If so, then it's just been made really easy, with this book you will immediately understand just how pervasive and important the social networks are going to become, and why you really need to care."
David Perry, Veteran Video Game Developer

"Jason and Jesse's I'm on Facebook—Now What? is a wonderful handbook for those who want to get the most out of their Facebook experience. Since they've been on the service for some time, they're bound to have discovered things everyday users haven't through regular surfing. For anyone who wondered, 'Now what?', or why people have been flocking to the social networking site, or what potential lies within for clubs and small businesses, the duo answer these questions in an easily digestible handbook."
Jack Yan, CEO, Jack Yan & Associates, Wellington, New Zealand, http://www.jackyan.com

Acknowledgements

I'd like to thank my family for supporting me on this second book (even after I swore I wouldn't do it again)—especially Kaisie, Samantha, William, Taylor and Kimberly. Also, to all of my colleagues, partners and champions, who have provided unending support during my career transition from happily employed to unhappily unemployed to happily self-employed. Finally, I'd like to thank Jesse, who willingly took on this project with excitement and vigor, and has proven to be the perfect coauthor.
Jason Alba

Thanks to my family, Elizabeth, Thomas, Joseph (and new baby on the way—whatever your name is!), and especially my dear wife Rebecca who, while pregnant and dealing with three kids, has gracefully endured my writing and starting a new business. I'd also like to thank my two youngest sisters, Michelle and Crystal, for giving me reason to join Facebook. Thanks to Scoble, Lorenzen, Pirillo, O'Neill, Brogan and countless others who have contributed to or aided in the writing of this book. Thanks to my coauthor Jason whose help and experience taught me how crazy authoring a book really is! Most of all, a special thank you to my fourth- and fifth-grade elementary school teachers, Mr. Reinsmoen and Mr. Denton. Without having had the patience to let me play with those old Apples in the back of their rooms, this book would not exist.
Jesse Stay

We would both like to publicly thank Apple for their commercial in which they help promote the "Now What???" books. You can see their attempt to mimic our clever title in this video: http://www.youtube.com/watch?v=kYoQ77tLeq8[1]

---

1. This URL is case sensitive. You can also see the video here: http://tinyurl.com/2xm3xq and here: http://tinyurl.com/22mo6r.

A Message from Happy About®

Thank you for your purchase of this Happy About book. It is available online at http://happyabout.info/facebook.php or at other online and physical bookstores.

- Please contact us for quantity discounts at sales@happyabout.info
- If you want to be informed by e-mail of upcoming Happy About® books, please e-mail us at bookupdate@happyabout.info

Happy About is interested in you if you are an author who would like to submit a non-fiction book proposal or a corporation that would like to have a book written for you. Please contact us by e-mail at editorial@happyabout.info or phone (1-408-257-3000).

Other Happy About books available include:

- I'm on LinkedIn--Now What???
  http://happyabout.info/linkedinhelp.php
- Internet Your Way to a New Job
  http://happyabout.info/InternetYourWaytoaNewJob.php
- The Emergence of the Relationship Economy
  http://happyabout.info/RelationshipEconomy.php
- Tales from the Networking Community
  http://happyabout.info/networking-community.php
- Awakening Social Responsibility
  http://happyabout.info/csr.php
- Scrappy Project Management
  http://happyabout.info/scrappyabout/project-management.php
- 42 Rules of Marketing
  http://happyabout.info/42rules/marketing.php
- Foolosophy
  http://happyabout.info/foolosophy.php
- The Home Run Hitter's Guide to Fundraising
  http://happyabout.info/homerun-fundraising.php
- Confessions of a Resilient Entrepreneur
  http://happyabout.info/confessions-entrepreneur.php
- Memoirs of the Money Lady
  http://happyabout.info/memoirs-money-lady.php
- 30-Day Bootcamp: Your Ultimate Life Makeover
  http://happyabout.info/30daybootcamp/life-makeover.php
- Rule #1: Stop Talking! A Guide to Listening
  http://happyabout.info/listenerspress/stoptalking.php
- Communicating the American Way
  http://happyabout.info/communicating-american-way.php

Contents

Foreword

I discovered Facebook and signed up in mid-June 2007. Prior to that time, I had heard some tidbits about it from my sons who were in college, but I didn't really understand what a social network was and all that I was missing. So, sadly for me, when I got started with Social Networking there was no book like *I'm on Facebook—Now What???*. If there had been, I would have been able to avoid a number of pitfalls and thus been able to take greater advantage of Facebook sooner.

Fortunately for you, you've discovered the roadmap that I didn't have.

As someone who has been in the software industry for 25+ years, I believe that an operating system revolution like Facebook comes around only so often. It was at the beginning of my career that Windows became the first mainstream Graphical Operating System, significantly changing the future of software creation, distribution and monetization. The advent of the Internet has had a similar impact over the past decade. Now, Facebook has emerged as the first mainstream *Social* Operating System and, I believe, will again significantly change the future of software creation, distribution and monetization.

Just like in 1998, when CEOs were asking themselves "What is our Internet strategy?" the question for businesses in 2008 will be "What is our Facebook strategy?"

My advice to anyone who is just discovering Facebook is to digest the information contained in this book and really explore all of the nooks and crannies of Facebook. This effort will be rewarded—not only on a personal basis via closer connections with your friends and family—but also on a business basis via closer connections with your customers.

In the personal realm, the applications on Facebook can turn your profile page into a "Bloomberg terminal for your life." You will use it every morning or even multiple times per day to keep track of your corner of the social graph. This is why, in the business realm, I say Facebook is the "lowest cost customer-acquisition vehicle on the planet."[2] It provides both global and local businesses with a new tool to help their businesses grow via not only word-of-mouth but also word-of-mouse.

In summary, I hope you enjoy the book as much as I did, and I also hope you join the 60 million Facebook users that were signed up as of Dec. 2007. If my predictions are right (see blog.adonomics.com) Facebook's active users will number more than 200 million by Dec. 2008 and Facebook's value will be at least $100 billion. This type of exponential growth is just one of the reasons why your investment in learning more about Facebook will provide you with one of your best returns ever.

Lee Lorenzen
CEO, Altura Ventures—the first Facebook-only VC

---

2.   http://blog.adonomics.com/2007/12/06/why-facebook-is-worth-100-billion.

Introduction

In 2007, Jason Alba wrote *I'm on LinkedIn—Now What???*[3] to help professionals understand the power of LinkedIn and figure out how they could derive personal career and professional benefits from LinkedIn. Instead of being a user manual or a technology guide, it is a book to help people figure out what LinkedIn means for them in practical terms.

That's exactly what this book is about—helping you figure out how to derive personal, business and career benefits from participating in Facebook. Since Jason has significantly less time and experience on Facebook than he has on LinkedIn, he found one of the leading Facebook experts to bring strong technical, marketing and user experience: Jesse Stay.

Jesse is one of those guys that grew up programming from an early age (10, to be exact). When Facebook opened up their development platform, he jumped on and brainstormed a few different ideas he thought would work well on the platform. One of his Applications was acquired within just two months. Let's put this into perspective: He had an idea, wrote the Application, marketed it on Facebook, got tens of thousands of users, and sold it to a third party, all within 60 days! Clearly, Jesse understands more than just the '1s' and '0s' of writing a Facebook Application!

---

3. http://www.ImOnLinkedInNowWhat.com.

So why a book on Facebook and not Xing, Ecademy, Rise, Orkut, Beebo, MySpace, ZoomInfo, Jobster, or any of the others?[4] Facebook is one of the fastest growing online communities. Lee Lorenzen valued Facebook at $100 billion dollars, attributing this valuation to (among other things) Facebook's tremendous growth and its flexible developer platform.[5] It's also a very exciting social network[6] that allows businesses and professionals an opportunity to promote their message, offering and brand to a wide professional audience. We're not writing this book because Facebook is huge, growing or popular. We're writing this book because Facebook is a tool for *you*, and we want to help you get the most out of it!

In addition to helping you understand what Facebook is, we'll provide examples, advice and **Action Items** to help you develop and execute a Facebook strategy for you or your company. We've reached out to dozens of social networking experts to see how they are using Facebook, what their top recommendations are, and what resources they find most valuable, and feel confident that you are getting advice from the best of the best.

One final note: Facebook is not LinkedIn and it's not MySpace. Each of the major networks have buzz and bling for various reasons, and understanding what Facebook can do for you is a requirement in today's business world—whether you are learning about Facebook for your company or for You, Inc.,[7] this book should be a great place to start!

Best Wishes,

Jason Alba
CEO
JibberJobber.com

Jesse Stay
Chief Social Officer, Partner
SocialOptimize.com

---

4. http://thevirtualhandshake.com/directory.html.
5. http://tinyurl.com/2zlxby.
6. Facebook calls itself a "social utility," which is obviously different, but in this book we'll just keep it simple by keeping it in the "social networking" category.
7. http://www.fastcompany.com/magazine/10/brandyou.html.

1 Getting Started

Facebook is a website that launched on February 4, 2004 (LinkedIn launched on May 5, 2003[8] and MySpace launched in August 2003) and has become one of the hottest websites in history, ranking with Google. Originally it was available only to Harvard students, then it opened to students at other colleges and universities. In September 2006 it was opened to any user with any email address,[9] 13 years of age or older. Having already been an immensely popular social network in the college space, Facebook's decision to open up to non-students was followed by a huge surge in users.

Almost overnight, and for a number of reasons, Facebook went from "college social networking" to something professionals wanted to be involved in. The primary reasons include:

First, Facebook has a huge user base. Of course MySpace has the biggest user base, with over 200 million people registered. At the time of this writing Facebook "only" has about 70 millions users.[10] That is still significantly larger than LinkedIn, which is approaching 20 million

---

8. http://tinyurl.com/34byyn
9. http://en.wikipedia.org/wiki/Facebook.
10. http://tinyurl.com/k2jhx.

users. Sure, each of the three networks has a lot of users, but it's worth mentioning that Facebook is not weak in this area.

Second, users are spending significant time on Facebook. Facebook provides enough coolness, fun and functionality that people can spend a lot of time on the site. And people do spend a lot of time on the site. TechCrunch wrote about a Facebook user who spent about 20 hours a week surfing around Facebook while working as a trader at Goldman Sachs! When he was called on it by the IT department, he posted a message on his Wall stating he was more interested in spending this much time on Facebook than he was keeping his job![11]

Third, the user demographics are quite different than what you see on MySpace or LinkedIn. LinkedIn has a reputation on the blog-osphere for serving primarily the 35-and-over market (but don't necessarily go by this—there are plenty of younger people who are, or should be, on LinkedIn). This is interesting because it connotes the working professional, established in their career. It also leaves out the entire Generation Y crowd, which is one of the hottest topics in workforce recruiting right now. Guess where they are? Yep, Facebook.

Fourth, Facebook has a history of introducing useful, enticing feature for the users. In just under a year, Facebook has launched a plethora of new features and continues to surprise us with more. Of the many features released, they have opened their network to non-college students, launched the News Feed of Friends activities, launched a developer platform, released Mobile features, introduced "Facebook Pages," and just recently added the option to group one's Friends. This list continues to grow, and will probably be larger by the time you read this.

TIP Visit the blog behind this book for current and updated information: http://www.FacebookAdvice.com.

Fifth, Facebook allows developers to create new Applications that users can add into their own Profile with few restrictions. This allows thousands of professionals to contribute to the richness of the Facebook experience, giving them vested interest in Facebook and

---

11. http://tinyurl.com/2cahx9.

their network, and even making some of them wealthy. While Facebook is sensitive to privacy issues, there are thousands of developers creating Facebook Applications, and although it's impossible to completely check every company or person, Applications are being added at a very fast pace.

We think the features of Facebook fall somewhere between what LinkedIn and MySpace provide. When you go there you won't be inclined to blush nearly as much as you might while surfing around MySpace—people tend to be less crude on Facebook. That's not to say that there aren't things that shouldn't be there—you'll still find quotes, pictures, Profiles, Groups and Applications that are likely to turn off a hiring employer, potential customer, business partner or someone's mom. But these are generally less frequent and more subdued than what you'll see on MySpace.

LinkedIn, on the other hand, doesn't have many of the social networking features, and it keeps itself at a professional level. You can think of your LinkedIn Profile as a resume, where you have the ability to allow others that you're connected with to endorse you (think of it as a very short letter of recommendation). One of the most social features on LinkedIn is "Answers," but there aren't other areas to collaborate, share, hang out, etc.

With the exciting features comes complexity. My landing page on Facebook looks quite cluttered, with Applications, blog posts from my Friends, introductions to Groups, Notices (who has a birthday coming up, who joined or left which Group, etc.) and more. I have my Wall, which is where anyone (including me) can write and see messages—kind of like a bulletin board. You'll see "happy birthday!!!" wishes more often than you'll see a professional endorsement on someone's Wall.

TIP Facebook is very sensitive to privacy issues but we think it's impossible to prevent any kind of abuse from Application developers. Facebook tries to check developers and Applications but it *is* possible that a rogue Application is made public. More on this in Chapter 5.

Navigating Facebook

Because Facebook is so feature-rich (between the core features and the Applications) you might feel overwhelmed by all of the things pulling at your attention. At the top of the screen you have the following navigation options:

Profile edit **Friends** ▼ **Networks** ▼ **Inbox (90)** ▼

Following is a basic breakdown of the main navigational options and what you might want to *pay attention to*:

Profile: The important things to know about in the Profile section include:

Home Page: Note that you can always get back to your Facebook Home Page by clicking on the Facebook logo. When you mouse over it, there's even a little blue home icon (kind of elusive, but just remember, click on "Facebook" to go Home).

Status: Home, work, at a party, with the family, sleeping (doesn't that sum up a college kids life?). Notice, there's no "doing home-work!" The very first option is a blank box—that's where you can write whatever you want, such as "on vacation," "making money," "in a job search," "in a boring meeting," etc.

TIP Easily update your status using Twitter (add the Twitter Application to your Facebook Profile).

Networks: This shows what Networks you belong to or might want to join. You can join multiple Networks with some considerations. You can be in only one geographic Network at a time. Also, in order to join a school or work Network, you must have a valid corre-sponding school or work e-mail address. This restriction is great for privacy, but doesn't help if you don't have access to the school or work e-mail account required for access to the network. For example, if you don't have an e-mail address from your alma mater, you can't join that group.

TIP Add your business as a Network.

Birthday: Once you get some Friends on Facebook you'll probably get some birthday well-wishes. This surprised Jason at first, to have people who shouldn't know what his birthday is, send him e-mails saying "happy birthday!". When they go into Facebook they can see a list of friends' upcoming birthdays.

TIP Add the fbCal Application to synchronize your Friends birthdays into your local calendar.

The image below shows the Profile options with all of the sections minimized (when you first arrive at the Profile Page, these sections are expanded, so it will be a long, busy page):

Jason Alba
is working on my book!
Updated 9 seconds ago edit

Networks:	Salt Lake City, UT
Sex:	Male
Birthday:	[will show month/day to your friends]
Hometown:	Herriman, UT

▶ Mini-Feed

▶ Information

▶ Work

▶ Jobster Career Network X

▶ Interactive Friends Graph X

▶ My Linkedin Power Forum X

The next section shows the Applications you have allows you to manage any Applications that you may have added.

The **Mini-Feed**[12] section will show you all the cool stuff you want to know, and lots you probably don't want to know. You can choose from eighteen different "stories" including Network, Relationship, Group,

Event, Photo, Note (blog entries), Posted Items, Video, Wall, etc. The list goes on and on.

The **Information** section is where you keep all your personal Profile data up to date. You can enter the following types of Profile information:

- *Basic information*—sex, birthday, hometown, political views, religious views.

- *Contact information*—phone, e-mail, physical address, website, chat services, etc.

- *Relationship information*—your relationship status (married, dating, and others, including "it's complicated"), maiden names (excellent feature—it doesn't show up on your Profile but it helps if people search for you), and what you are looking for. Being the married men that we are, we checked "networking" and left the others blank!

- *Personal information*—a bunch of boxes where you can enter what your interests are including activities, favorite music, TV shows, movies, books, etc.

- *Education*—enter the college(s) and high school(s) you attended.

- *Work*—enter your current and past employers.

- *Your picture*—you get only one Profile picture, but you can have up to 60 pictures in your Profile Picture Album.

- *Layout*—actually doesn't do anything except tell you that you can change the layout of your Profile Page and drag things around.

Friends: Allows you to see your Friends. It defaults to display only your Friends who have recently updated their Profile, but you can jump around and see Friends based on other criteria (e.g., who is currently online, who is in your Network, and so on.)

Network: The easiest Network to join is based on geography (where you live). Beyond that, you can find Networks related to work, high school or college. Again, you need a valid e-mail address to join a school (college or university) or work Network, and probably have to

---

12. http://www.facebook.com/minifeed.php.

have a special link to join a high school Network. You can only join one geographic Network at a time—if you try to join a second one you will have to leave the first one.

When you click to join a Network you get this notice: "Once you join, you will be able to see the profiles of other people in the Provo, Utah Network, and they will be able to see yours. You can change your privacy settings on the Privacy page."

Inbox: This is the place to find all of the messages that people send you through Facebook. Some people seem to think using the Inbox is better than sending you an e-mail, which is a pain if you already have an e-mail management strategy. Nonetheless, it is worthwhile to check every once in a while and clean out your Inbox, as you're likely to find some messages that need a response.

Simply understanding the links and navigation tools throughout Facebook will help you get more out of your experience, as well as know where to go to do certain things.

ACTION ITEMS

- Click through each of the main links and poke around, especially looking for settings that you should change.

- Set up your account (if you don't have one already).

- If you have anything in your Inbox, clean it out (one by one, so you can understand what kinds of things end up in an Inbox).

- Set up your Profile options and your Mini-Feed.

- Fill out your work and education history.

- Fill out your contact information (keep in mind that only those people who add you as a Friend on Facebook can see this).

- Upload a Profile photo of yourself.

- Select a Network to join.

QUOTES FROM FACEBOOK USERS

"Job hunting these days is all about being found online and creating a digital profile for employers to find you. Most companies are now researching candidates before and after the interview so it's in your best interest to give them something positive to read. Keep your Facebook profile updated, especially the Education and Work sections."

Chris Russell
http://www.secretsofthejobhunt.com

"How to edit the News Feed is important. I hate seeing all the applications that people add, so I turned those people off. When you are on the home page click preferences, which is on the same line as the header new feed. You'll get a picture of something that looks like an equalizer board. It's very useful with filtering out general things. It also has the ability to let you choose which people you want to see less/more information about."

Dorothy Taffet
UCONN

2 Getting Involved

In addition to just having an account and setting up your Profile, there are various things to do to get involved in this social network. This chapter explains what you should do to increase your exposure and reach to your Network, and their Networks.

Connecting with Others— Facebook Friends

Facebook connections are called "Friends." Where LinkedIn suggests that you only connect with people you "know and trust," Facebook Friend connections are generally a lot looser. In other words, being connected really means different things on each Network. Sure, a connection is some kind of tie between two people, granting some level of access to one another's Networks and Profile. But the social and privacy issues surrounding Facebook Friends and LinkedIn connections are quite different.

For instance, being connected on LinkedIn allows your connection(s) to browse (or search through) your network. When you are connected, you are able to see one another's connections. It also means that if you ask a question on "Answers," or want to send an update to your connections, you may get an e-mail (based on your preferences). When you login to LinkedIn, you see a summary of what your network is up to, including who is growing their network, who has asked or answered questions, etc. But that's about it.

Being your Facebook Friend gives us a lot more insight into what's going on with you. This is why people say they use LinkedIn to stay in touch with business contacts, whereas they use Facebook to stay in touch with their social contacts, or to keep updated on what's going on with their Network contacts.

When we login to Facebook we see a long list of news from people in our Network. Whether it's a blog post that they just put up, pictures, videos, and their Status with Groups (leaving or joining) and Applications, we get a pretty good view of what our Friends are doing. We love the birthday reminder, telling us who has an upcoming birthday, almost giving us a nudge to reach out and say "happy birthday!"

It seems that many Facebook users are using Facebook as their Internet browser, spending so much time on it that they don't really go to other sites to get what they need—they can get it all within Facebook!

Who should you connect with? It's up to you, but consider this: If you want to know what's going on with another person, or you want to communicate an upcoming event with another person, make sure you are connected to that person.

For example, when Jason learned that his friend, Andy Sernovitz,[13] was coming to speak on Word of Mouth Marketing in Salt Lake City, he immediately thought of ways to advertise. In addition to the typical methods of marketing such an event (blog posts, e-mails, press releases, etc.), he set up a Facebook Event. About ten percent of Jason's Facebook Network is in Utah, so he was able to immediately communicate details of the Event to about eighteen people.

Imagine if Jason had one hundred local Friends, or one hundred marketing and public relations Friends, or one hundred student and

---

13. http://damniwish.com.

professor Friends? In figuring out who you want to connect with, ask yourself who you may want to communicate with in the future. This advice goes for other social networks as well. Always consider Network contact types by:

* *Geography*—city, county, state, region, etc.

* *Industry*—marketing, internet, retail, coaching, consulting, religion, political, etc.

* *Profession*—web programmer, word of mouth expert, writer, editor, blogger, teacher, accountant, etc.

* *Interest*—skier, runner, racer, voracious reader, sci-fi lover, etc.

This is one of the most important decisions you'll make as it will affect the types of communications you get and the ways you can communicate with others.

Using the Andy Sernovitz visit as an example, here's a bonus idea: When Jason created the Event and e-mailed the eighteen people in his geographic Network that match the geographic type of requirements (this event was limited to those who could physically attend), then each time any of those people confirmed they would be attending, their Networks might see it on their own landing page (depending on their News Feed settings). This is a great way to help spread the word about an event!

Once you start connecting with various people you'll get invitations to connect from others based solely on the statement "we have a friend in common." This seems to be against LinkedIn policy, but commonplace (and acceptable) in Facebook. Is that okay? We think so!

Scott Allen, author of *The Virtual Handshake,*[14] differentiates the types of connections he has on each Network based on the kind of networking each promotes (Scott writes about this, with a strong emphasis on his LinkedIn strategy).[15] You should do what you are comfortable with, and you certainly don't want to create more work for yourself (managing the number of Group invitations and communications can be a burden), but being connected to people that are movers and

---

14. http://thevirtualhandshake.com.
15. http://www.linkedintelligence.com/my-linkedin-connection-policy.

shakers in your space (including geographic, industry, profession or interest) can really be worth it.

Once you have friends on Facebook you'll see news and information about them on your landing page, and they can see news and information about you when they login, too! Here is a checklist of the default settings that you are showing to them (and conversely, that they are showing you) on each of your respective landing pages:

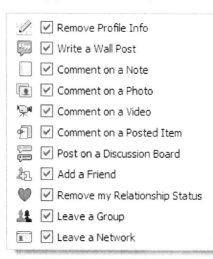

In addition to each of these activities that you are showing your Facebook Friends, and activities you'll see about your Facebook Friends, you will also show/ see when a Profile is edited, when a Network is joined, when a Status is changed, and more.

Below are some examples (names changed for privacy reasons):

We saw the first example on the News Feed after a friend went to a basketball game, which was an Event in Facebook. The second example is because two Friends added the Sketch Me Application. By default, you are showing your Friends most of the activity you do within

Facebook, including when you add Applications, join or leave Groups, say you are going to attend an Event, etc. (However, you are not showing them where you *go* in Facebook, for example; when you check out Groups but don't join them.)

It's fun to see what others are doing, but eerie at the same time to know that they might see almost everything you, too, are doing on Facebook! Are you comfortable showing everything you do via your Friends' landing page? Before you answer that, consider the origins of Facebook. It started in a university setting, where displaying things like this is cool and socially acceptable. The word "transparent" comes to mind.

There's more information about privacy and security in Chapter 5, but let's keep this in perspective. We're not saying that it's good or even okay to publicize all of this information, and different people will have different comfort levels, so you need to figure out what *your* comfort level is. As you add Friends on Facebook, you are welcoming them into your world in a big way, at least with all of the privacy settings turned on (which is the default).

The Friend List feature allows you to create lists and then add Friends to the lists. You can group your Friends into different demographics such as "friends", "family", "competitors", "customers", "Professors", etc.

You can use a Friend List in messages sent from Facebook Mail, Notes and Applications you share, etc.

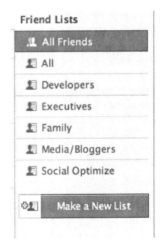

Grouping Your Facebook Friends into Friend Lists

For example, for the Facebook Page[16] for this book, Jesse used his Friend Lists. He sent one message to each Executive in his list, a different message to friends and family, and another message to bloggers and media.

This new feature offers a lot of business potential. We hope this feature gets incorporated into the privacy features of Facebook to allow more targeted communication. For example, it would be powerful to allow certain lists to see a particular type of status message or News Feed update, and other lists to see other types of status messages or News Feed updates.

Facebook Groups

There are over ten thousand Facebook Groups you can join. In just a few minutes of browsing the Groups, you'll find that many are pretty silly, especially the ridiculously popular Groups. While you might not be interested in joining the "Bug Me During Grey's Anatomy And I'll Insert This Scalpel Into Your Spleen"[17] Group (117,730 members), you may want to join the "Fans of MarketingProfs"[18] Group (well over 600 members), especially if you are a marketer (or an aspiring marketer)!

TIP To expand your reach and visibility, join Groups in which you have an associated interest.

Groups that might be worth your time include those created for your company or school (high school, university, etc.), Groups initiated by bloggers or authors, or special interest Groups. You can easily search for Groups by putting in keywords that relate to industry, profession, location, etc.

One thing to consider, aside from finding Groups to join, is to start your own Group. Check out some Groups that have a purpose similar to yours and learn from them. For example, as we were writing this book we found various Groups by authors. When people joined the Group they would be informed of Group news, which essentially became a very convenient mailing list for the Group admin. In addition, Group

16. http://www.facebook.com/profile.php?id=6816644117.
17. http://www.facebook.com/group.php?gid=2206195283.
18. http://www.facebook.com/group.php?gid=19230516048.

members have the ability to add pictures, write on the Wall and do all the things you can do on a profile, if the Group admin allows you to.

When you make Friends or join Groups, expect to start getting e-mails or notifications related to the Group. These range from lame to useful, depending on your interest level. As a Group owner, be careful to respect the way people want to receive communication. For example, we prefer getting e-mail notifications with the content in the e-mail, and not have to login to a website to see what the message is all about. This means you may want to consider a complementary communication tool such as a Yahoo! or Google Group.

Let's use the "Fans of MarketingProfs" to illustrate some of the finer features of Facebook Groups. If you go to this Group you'll see features similar to what you would see on a Profile Page. For example, you can see content posted by Group members on the Wall, pictures and videos (no videos in the Marketing Profs Group yet). You can click a link to "see all" of the 600+ Group members. Browsing through the list of Group members is a great way to learn about others, and can help you find new contacts to invite as your own Facebook Friends.

Staying in Touch

On the right side of the screen you'll see requests, notifications, updates and more. Most of these things you will also see when you click the Inbox link at the top of the screen. Instead of immediately acting on any invitation or notice that lands in your e-mail, you can check periodically to see what may be accumulating here. We don't like to interrupt our workflow and immediately accept a Friends invitation, so we'll just check our Inbox the next time we login.

It's easy to see how many Friend requests you have by looking on the right side of the screen, as opposed to going to the Facebook Inbox, since it tells you how many invitations you have received to be a Friend, join an Event or Group, try out an Application, etc. You will also notice that once you start adding new Applications, you may see new Notices under the Invitations area.

Can you ignore or deny or reject any of these invitations? Sure! Jason ignores them all the time! Jason is pretty liberal on the Friend invitations and very conservative on the Group invitations (read: he ignores almost all Group invitations). He is not interested in causes as he doesn't really think that joining a cause on Facebook is going to change the world... He's looking for things to do here that will have a positive impact on his business or career, and Vampire and Zombie invitations would more likely have a negative impact on a business or career!

Feel free to ignore invitations. We give you permission!

ACTION ITEMS

- Search for some friends, colleagues or college roommates to add as Friends, and add them.

- Join at least one of the Groups that you have an interest in—you can search for things such as programmer, project manager, accountant, etc. and will likely find at least one Group that should catch your eye.

- Again, check your Inbox to see if there is anything that you should attend to.

- Invite five people to be your Friend on Facebook.

- Create an Event on Facebook, even if you aren't hosting it. If you can't think of an event, now's a great time to have a dinner party or something like that.

- Look through your Friends' Friends to see if there are people *you* should add as Friends.

- Find the Advanced Search Page and do some specific searches such as "CEO" and the name of your town.

QUOTES FROM FACEBOOK USERS

"Take the time to accurately fill in your Friend details for how you know a person. Often someone will friend me after reading my blog post or seeing me on Twitter, but I don't know them [yet!]. Friend details are an easy way to refresh my memory when we interact in the future, and save an awkward 'How do I know you again?' moment."

Marina Martin
Owner, TypeAs, Inc.
http://www.TypeAs.com

Facebook provides an incredible amount of opportunities, but it's really all about connections. Sure it's a good place to share pictures, and some of the applications are a lot of fun, but without those connections, there would be nothing.

Matt J McDonald
A New Marketing
http://www.anewmarketing.com

3 Commonly Asked Questions

As we reached out to our friends and network contacts to ask for input and feedback for this book, we received a lot of questions and concerns. By far, the most popular questions were about the differences between Facebook and LinkedIn, where many people felt that Facebook was for the younger crowd and LinkedIn was for the professional, business crowd.

While we can't dispute the differences in philosophy, features and user demographics, we feel strongly that each platform provides excellent networking, business and career development opportunities. Does that mean Facebook is right for you? Perhaps not, but we think if you step back and look at the pros and cons of having an account and participating in certain ways, you will see there is considerable opportunity to use Facebook as a communications tool. Below are some of the commonly asked questions we've seen, and each question is followed by our commentary. Note that answers to these questions can be found in more detail throughout this book.

What is the difference between Facebook and LinkedIn (read: Why would I use Facebook and/or LinkedIn)?

LinkedIn is a place to find and be found, with few opportunities for interaction. You go there to set up a professional profile and *use* the search tools to find people that may be helpful in your career, job or business. It's a powerful tool, of course, but it differs from Facebook dramatically.

Facebook has, at the time of this writing, more than three times the number of users as LinkedIn. Facebook has a heavy user base of younger, college-age members, who started their accounts for the purpose of social networking rather than business or professional networking. With this in mind, features are geared more towards social networking. However, changes in the last eighteen months have altered the landscape, and it has evolved into something that experts are more often comparing to LinkedIn (we still think there's plenty of room for both platforms).

Isn't Facebook just for social/college networking?

That's how it started out, limiting sign-ups to those with a ".edu" e-mail address. With changes in 2006, allowing anyone with an e-mail address to sign up, we began to see many non-students come in looking for opportunities (opportunities to hook up, find business, see what all the buzz was about, or just poke around). But it's still hard to get over the reputation of those early days when people thought it was just for college kids.

Can I really further my career on Facebook like I can on LinkedIn?

Of course. Hiring managers, HR and recruiters may check your Facebook Profile to learn more about you. Additionally, career management has a lot to do with network relationships, and Facebook is a networking platform. Sure there are people who have objectionable material in their account, but that doesn't mean you have to. Learn where Facebook can help enhance your network relationships and it can serve as a very useful career tool. In addition, there are job postings and company-sponsored "Pages" on Facebook, hoping to lure new talent.

Is it ready for business/professional networking yet?

This goes back to the question, "Isn't Facebook only for social/college networking?" Clearly, if you work for a company that is interested in the college market, then you need to have been on Facebook yesterday! Did you know that 'the fastest growing demographic [in Facebook] is 25 years and older?'[19] You aren't going to find all of the professional networking tools that you find on LinkedIn but, even so, there is still immense opportunity. You just have to know what to do and how to do it right. Remember, HR and hiring managers will frequently look for candidate Profiles on Facebook.

What the heck is a Poke?

From the Help Page: "People interpret the Poke in many different ways, and we encourage you to come up with your own meanings." When you Poke someone, "a Poke icon will appear on his or her Home Page with the option to 'Remove Poke' or 'Poke Back'." So the Poke does nothing more than just put a little Notice on their Home Page, kind of like "I've been thinking about you." Don't waste your time on this—if you want to reach out to someone, reach out to them. If you get Poked you can Poke back, but don't feel obligated to.

Question on Applications and privacy—Can you add an Application if you don't check all five checkboxes??

When you want to add a new Application you are first presented with a few checkbox items to consider. One of these, "Know who I am and access my information," must be checked. The others are optional:

---

19. http://www.facebook.com/press/info.php?statistics.

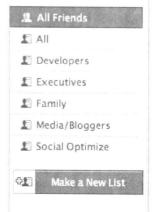

Friend Lists

The issue here is privacy, so realize that when you allow the Application to "know who [you are] and access [your] information," you are granting access to a third party to have a lot of access to your Profile data. Privacy is one of the hottest Facebook topics around.

Is there a limit to the number of contacts I can have, and is there talk about lifting this limit?

The limit to the number of Friends you can have in Facebook is 5,000. In fact, the term "whale" has been used to refer to those who have thousands of connections.[20] This is disconcerting to those on LinkedIn who have way more than 5,000 connections. As recent at October, 2007, Robert Scoble talks about this limit and presents some excellent points—one of our favorite points is that real friends and Facebook Friends are two different things. You can read more about this limit on Scoble's post,[21] as well as his thoughts and input from dozens of readers.

What sections of Facebook are people using??

According to the Compete website analytics statistics,[22] the most popular things to do on Facebook are browse Profiles, browse Pictures, and interact with Applications. It is therefore no surprise that Applications are so popular, especially when you consider the usefulness that Applications add to the Facebook experience. The idea that people use Facebook and spend a significant amount of time on it means there is a lot of opportunity to find and build relationships—is your Profile fleshed out? Do you have a nice picture attached to it?

---

20. http://rob.orangejack.com/2007/07/25/are-you-a-facebook-whale/.
21. http://scobleizer.com/2007/10/14/the-you-dont-need-more-friends-lobby/.
22. http://blog.compete.com/2007/09/14/facebook-activity-breakdown-application/.

How can I use Facebook to market my products/services?

You can let your Friends know what you are up to, and create buzz around your interests. For example, you can feed your blog posts and Twitter tweets to your Friends so that when they login, they see what's new. You can post YouTube and Flickr content which goes straight to their landing page (as long as their privacy settings allow that). Jens Berget, author of the Sly Marketing blog, has a great post[23] on this very topic (note the related posts, where he has some other very relevant how-to's about Facebook).

What are the most important things I must do on Facebook to ensure it is useful for me?

In order to answer this question you need to define "useful." For some it simply means expanding a network, for others it means moving product. We strongly encourage you to spend about an hour to put together your Profile to make sure that when people come to your Page they can learn what's important about you. Set up your privacy settings appropriately, see what Applications your Friends are using, write on some Walls, share some pictures, and generally get involved in Facebook. That way, when people come across your Profile they'll see that you didn't just sign in and then go away. If you want to leave it at that, that's fine. Otherwise, you can get more involved, work to grow your Network, set up Events (on-site, webinars, teleseminars, etc.), join and setup Groups, etc. If you want to create buzz you have to be out there growing your network.

Is anyone legitimately making money on Facebook, or using it for business?

Facebook is making money, that's clear. They have an advertising model and, believe it or not, there are people who will buy a $1 virtual gift (ranging from roses to a beer) for their Friends. Individuals are making money on Facebook, too. Here are some examples:

With over 400,000 members, Barack Obama's One Million Strong for Barack Group has a link for making donations. Aside from financial do-

---

23. http://www.slymarketing.com/2007/10/facebook-status/.

nations, though, voters can see that this candidate has something in common with them (in addition to his Group, he has an Application to keep up-to-date on the race), and there is strong support. You can find similar Groups for other presidential candidates, local city counsel hopefuls, and so on.

Recruiters are also interested in Facebook, although many still favor LinkedIn to find passive candidates. But people *are* finding jobs through Facebook, which means recruiters are making placements (and getting paid).

There are thousands of independent Facebook developers and consultants (including Jesse's company), and tens of thousands of Applications. Some Applications have been purchased (acquired), with prices ranging from a few thousand to several million dollars.

There are still thousands of people wondering how to monetize this system, their networks, and the potential to create huge followings in Groups or Applications.

ACTION ITEMS

- Explain the business or professional benefits of a Facebook account to someone (don't preach or convince, this is an exercise to learn).

- Visit our website, http://.FacebookAdvice.com, for more links, updates and information for you and your Facebook strategy.

- Post an ad on Facebook. For about $5-$10 a day you can post an ad to a very small demographic—do this to see the power of Facebook advertising.

- Ask your Friends how they use Facebook—share their stories on our website!

- Ask questions on the "I'm on Facebook—Now What???" Facebook page.[1]

- Check out "I'm on LinkedIn—Now What???" and figure out a strategy using Facebook and LinkedIn together.

1.http://www.facebook.com/profile.php?id=6816644117.

QUOTES FROM FACEBOOK USERS

"Since connecting with Facebook back in the Summer of 2007 it has totally changed my life and the way I conduct business. I host events for media & entertainment executives here in the NYC area and Facebook has become a valuable tool on a variety of levels. In addition to allowing me to promote and market my events and related activities, it has become a wonderful way for people from all over the world to meet me, ask for advice and get connected with others on my Network. I have also been able to connect related organizations in a way that allows each of us to maintain our independence while at the same time cross-promote common causes and activities."

Bill Sobel
Chief Connections Officer
http://www.nymieg.org

"In the end Facebook, like other online social networking sites, is just a tool to help you make, keep and grow your business and personal relationships. It is up to you how you use this tool. If you are interested in the power of networking, then you must be online."

Thom Singer
Author/Speaker
http://www.thomsinger.com

4 Facebook Applications

What's the Deal with all the Facebook Applications Hype?

Since the F8 announcement,[24] opening up development to anyone who had the skills, application developers and businesses alike have gone gaga over writing Facebook Applications. Not since the dot-com boom have developers and businesses rushed to be the first to make their millions off a single platform. We understand the buzz, as Applications are generating millions of users in a matter of days. You can't deny that this mad rush, whether bust or boom, is at least something worth paying attention to.

While there are plenty of fun, silly or useless Applications, there are a lot of business-related Applications—and room for more. We'll talk about some of the issues around these business Applications, which may help you determine whether this is a direction you should go.

With over 70,000,000 users and a very targeted demographic, writing your own Application to

---

24. http://developers.facebook.com/videos.php.

integrate your brand may be a wise choice to consider. Applications that are popular on Facebook can quickly generate new users you may not have found outside of Facebook. A simple Facebook Application is fairly easy to develop, and gives your brand or website immediate viral and permissions marketing capabilities. Some advantages Applications offer include:

Immediately co-brand your product—Facebook gives you a way to quickly enter a very large community of individuals who may not have had exposure to your brand before. Writing an Application within Facebook opens your brand to a new audience, and gives further opportunities for interaction with your brand by users within this sub-community. With the added viral opportunities Facebook gives you, your brand has the chance to spread, at a relatively low cost!

Lead Generation—this is not an easy thing to do on Facebook, since Facebook is kind of a "mini-internet" of sorts. Users don't like to leave Facebook—they prefer to do their business only in Facebook if they can. However, with proper strategy, it can be possible to lead people from Facebook to your brand outside of Facebook. The popular Application "iLike" does this by letting you add a plug-in to your iTunes which keeps track of the songs you are listening to and shares them with your Friends. Even this integrates back to Facebook, however. One idea to get lead generation outside of Facebook is to develop your external website/application such that Facebook users will see a look similar to what they see on Facebook.

Advertising Opportunities—some of the most creative advertising opportunities we have seen have been designed with Facebook Applications. Because of the social nature of Facebook, added to the capability to generate 100% revenue from the Applications you develop in Facebook, a new generation of "social ads" has developed. For example, your Application can allow your users to forward information about your products to their Friends! The Application owner can track when items are purchased, then notify Friends of the application's Users that a product has been purchased. This may encourage their Friends to purchase the Product, or even add the application to their own account! The opportunities are endless when given full access to the Social Graph[25] within Facebook.

Aside from building an Application, you can use those that others have written for your own business—for instance, to allow your employees to synchronize and keep track of clients. While some IT departments block Facebook, it can actually be a valuable time-saver if used correctly. Here are a few of our favorite Applications for business users:

Linking Universe—Linking Universe is one of the coolest business Applications we have seen on Facebook. Linking Universe is built around a method to define the quality, not just quantity, of your Facebook Friends. They search your Friends list and, through a number of factors, assign a score as to how substantive those Friends are towards a business relationship. Along with that, they provide tools to create a business Profile for you, a resume, a play on the "SuperPoke!" Application geared towards businesses ("shake hands with [so and so]"), and even a CRM tool that integrates with your Facebook Friends, allowing you to track your interactions with them and others.

Twitter—Twitter is a great networking tool. It's also a great way to log what you are doing in life. There is a Twitter sub-application that allows you to update your Facebook Status each time you "tweet."

PayPal—PayPal displays a widget on your Profile that allows you to withdraw money you have earned from sales, have others pay you, or raise money via your Profile. This can be an excellent way to raise money for a cause your company is interested in, or perhaps allow your clients to pay you for services rendered.

Feedheads—this is a favorite among many Facebookers. Feedheads shares your favorite feeds from Google Reader and NewsGator with your Friends on Facebook—a great way to share your interests.

Mobile—Facebook Mobile allows you to send and receive Status updates, photos, videos, Wall posts and notifications, directly via your mobile phone. Also, by going to m.facebook.com on your mobile phone (with an internet connection, of course), you are presented with a mobile-friendly version of the site.

My Questions—the My Questions Application allows you to post questions to your Facebook Friends for them to answer. It's a great

---

25. http://blogs.zdnet.com/BTL/?p=5156.

tool to survey your friends, coworkers, clients, etc. for marketing, product reviews, industry issues, and other interests.

Here are some ways to use Facebook in a business environment with the appropriate Applications:

Tracking What Coworkers and Employees are Doing—when you befriend your coworkers and employees, you'll have a view into what they are doing. You can see when they add the Werewolf and Vampire Applications, which hopefully is not during work hours. But having access to messages they're posting on potential clients Walls, conferences they are attending, Groups they are following (that also may be of interest to you), or even photos from the latest company party is powerful. All of these things can help you stay current with what the rest of the company is doing. The Applications listed earlier are also great tools for keeping track of each other.

TIP Add coworkers, customers and vendors as Friends.

Improve Intra-Company Communications—encouraging your employees to post their primary goal for the day on their Status section can be a great way to know the priorities of your employees. Posting documentation as Notes and links can be a great way to share information. Using Applications such as Feedhead to share important news and research can improve employee knowledge. Using My Questions to post surveys among your employees can be a great way to gain insight into their opinions. Be careful though—always be aware that other Friends outside of the company can see what you are posting!

Using Facebook Pages to Promote Your Brand—Applications and Pages can make an excellent pair when used together correctly. Similarly to a Facebook Profile, an Application has the capability to display information differently if it is on a Page. For example, you can provide dynamic information that is stored on your server(s), such as a News Feed. We have a Facebook Page for this book, which is a great example of how to sell products (or services) in Facebook. (Look up Jesse's "Pokket" E-Commerce Application, which he hopes to release shortly after this book is published.)

Of course, there are a number of ways to use Facebook to enhance your career, nurture relationships, or for a job search. While the resume and job tracking functionalities are not directly built in, networking is, so you can add the ability to broadcast one's knowledge of career expertise right through the News Feed. By synching your blog with Facebook Notes, for example, every blog post you make gets broadcast to your Friends' News Feeds. So, add Friends that work at places you want to work for, start blogging, participate in relevant Groups, etc. and you can develop a strong business identity through Facebook.

You also establish an identity by the Applications you install. Keep in mind that your Profile may be the first impression someone gets of you, so be careful when choosing the Applications you install and allow onto your Profile (you can turn off the Profile box). Having a bunch of Vampires and Werewolves, or Ninjas and Pirates on your Profile Page may do more harm than good. We try to be very conscientious about adding only the Applications that are useful. This is one way to help ensure others have the best impression when they find our Profiles.

Here are some Applications you should know about for personal career management:

- *Facebook Mobile*—adds a cool feature when you activate it, listing the cell phone numbers of all your Facebook Friends. This can be a great "phone book" to rely on if you ever need to call someone in your circle of Friends.

- *HobNob!*—brings LinkedIn-like features into Facebook's viral features. Basically, you post someone you would like to get in touch with, and HobNob! will broadcast that name to your Friends and Friends of Friends until, hopefully, someone finds the person you are looking for.

How to Find Applications

With over ten thousand Applications to choose from, how do you find the right ones to add? There are several options available to you, depending on how specific and what type of search you want to perform. Of course, you always have the option, through your News

Feed, of just following what your Friends install, assuming your Friends are somewhat using or endorsing them.

The Facebook Applications Directory is the main index of all Applications written. To get on the directory, your Application must have more than five users and have been reviewed by Facebook. To access the directory, click the "Applications" link in the left column, then click "Browse More Applications."

Type in the name of an Application you are looking for, or a keyword of a type of Application, and it will display Application(s) along with the number of users who have added it, as well as Groups and Pages that are using it. This can be a great way to find something if you don't want to spend time surfing through the entire list of Applications in the Applications Directory.

Another way to find Applications is with Appsaholic. Appsaholic started as an external website which crawled Facebook's Applications Directory and stored statistics about each of the Applications it discovered. Eventually, it was converted into a regular Facebook Application which anyone can add to their Profile. Appsaholic allows you to specify multiple Applications at a time, compares them with each other, and even tries to assign a monetary value to each Application. It's a great Application to install if you want to learn what the top used Applications are, or track your or your competitor's Applications. To find it, just search for "Appsaholic" on Facebook.

TIP Look in your News Feed to see which applications your Friends have installed.

These are the top five Applications[26] on Facebook in Daily Active Users[27] (surprisingly, they all come from just two companies, Slide and RockYou!):

1. **Super Wall** (RockYou!): "Super Wall lets you write messages, post photos, and post videos on your wall."

2. **Fun Wall** (Slide: "FUN Wall! The name says it all! Videos, FunPix, Graffiti and more!"

3. **Top Friends** (Slide): "Save time and show your friends some love. Add a box of up to 32 of your BFFs to your profile. Now they are one click away, you don't have to search every time you want to go check up on them. Now the question is... who is in your top friends box?"

4. **Super Poke!** (Slide): "Why just poke when you can pinch, hug, tickle, pwn[28] or even throw sheep?"

5. **X Me** (RockYou!): "Tired of just poking? X Me opens up a whole new world of action-based messaging, for example 'Hug Her, Slap Him, Tickle Them!'"

---

26. Based on Appsaholic statistics at the time of this writing.
27. They are the most actively used Applications, not just installed.
28. http://en.wikipedia.org/wiki/Pwn.

These are some of our favorite Applications:

1. **Twittervision:** we are big Twitter users (Look us up! JesseStay and jasonalba). The Twittervision application communicates with Twittervision.com to keep track of the location you last Twittered *from*. By entering "L: (location)" into Twitter, it automatically positions your Twitter post ("tweet") on a digital map, which the Twittervision Application conveniently displays on your Profile. There is also a Twitter Application we use to update our Facebook Status directly from Twitter.

2. **Grand Central:** Jesse is biased about this one because, well, he wrote it! You basically insert your CallMe Button code from the popular GrandCentral.com, and it displays the "Call Me" button on your Profile so other users can easily call you without revealing your phone number. Try it on Jesse's Facebook profile[29] and leave him a message!

3. **We're Related:** Paul Allen, founder of Ancestry.com, put together this cool Application to help you keep track of your family on Facebook. It will automatically try to detect your family members on Facebook. You can also manually (or automatically, through a file standard called GEDCOM) enter your living and deceased family members. It also allows you to track family news, birthdays, and even have your own message board for your family members to communicate through.[30]

4. **Radical Buy:** said to be the next thing to put eBay out of business, Radical Buy allows you to post an item you want to sell, allowing you to offer a commission if others want to sell it from their Profile Page. The person who sells the item gets the commission, and you ship it to the buyer. Radical Buy seems to be at the core of what Social E-Commerce is becoming.

5. **iLike:** Jesse swore, because of the general popularity of iLike, that he would not install it. However, at the request of a client, he tried it one day and he now admits it may be his favorite Application on Facebook! Basically, iLike lets you choose your favorite music, then share that music with your Friends. There are Forums for artists and users to talk about their favorite artists. U2

---

29. http://www.facebook.com/profile.php?id=683545112.
30. Jesse consulted on the original Design for the "We're Related" Facebook Application.

even released an exclusive track through the Forums. You can purchase music directly from within iLike, which will redirect you to your favorite music store (such as iTunes). iLike allows you to download a plug-in for iTunes, which then tracks what you're listening to in iTunes and posts the information to your Profile. It also lets you view, directly within iTunes, what your Friends are currently listening to, as well as who else is listening to the music you are currently playing.

6. **Holy Rolls:** another Application Jesse is biased towards (because he wrote it!), Holy Rolls is a series of religious Applications allowing you to identify with your religion on Facebook. These Applications randomly display scriptures of your choosing, keep track of your Friends who are also part of your religion, and have specific features to make it more relevant to that religion. Currently there is a Catholic Application (We're Catholic), a Baptist Application (We're Baptist), an LDS Application (The LDS Application), with more religions applications coming. (Jesse no longer owns the LDS Application.)

One of the most valuable secrets held by successful Application developers on Facebook is how to market their Applications in a way that can generate millions of users in a matter of days. While it is possible, it takes considerable effort. Here are some techniques we suggest:

- *Post on the Directory*—you must have five Friends add the Application in order to post on the Directory, but once you do, this can be one of your most influential steps toward helping new users find your Application.

- *Include Search Terms in the Application's Title*—yes, Social Network Optimization (SNO) and Search Engine Optimization (SEO) can work together! By including specific search terms in your Application's title, it will appear higher in Facebook search results. The title also gets indexed in external search engines (Google, Yahoo, etc.) and will, therefore, show up in those search results, which is a great way to encourage non-Facebook users to join Facebook and install your Application.

- *Write an Invitation Page!*—this is the single most important thing you can do when you write your Application. In fact, it should be the first Page your users see when they add the Application. For instance, in promoting the Holy Rolls Applications, Jesse found this to be the most significant viral marketing tactic. Keep your Invitation Page in a prominent place and find ways to keep referring your users to it so they can invite their Friends. For example, using Notifications.

- *Use Notifications*—another very important step. This is where you encourage users to invite their Friends without realizing they are inviting them. For example, when you add the SuperPoke! Application and Poke your Friends, they are prompted to Poke you back, but they must install SuperPoke! before they can—and Super-Poke! gets another user!

- *Write News Feed templates (and use them!)*—these are templates you can send to Facebook to place around specific news items that you want your Application to send to another user's News Feed (landing page). Of course, it can't be guaranteed that this item will appear, but it is a terrific opportunity to virally encourage users' Friends to add your Application.

- *Have your servers ready!*—one of the biggest surprises that successful Application developers face is the sudden onslaught of traffic they get when thousands, or even millions, of users add their Application. Your Application is not hosted in Facebook's server environment, so be sure your hosting service provider can easily scale at a low cost. Two excellent services for this are Joyent Hosting, which has partnered with Facebook to guarantee traffic, and Amazon Elastic Compute Cloud (EC2) combined with Amazon S3. Both scale very well *and* are very affordable options for a high-traffic Application.

TIP Seek patent protection if you are concerned about your application data.

ACTION ITEMS

- Look for, and add, three Applications to your own account.

- Look for an Application from a competitor or someone in your industry, and figure out what value they are offering to Facebook members.

- Determine three benefits/values to offer people who would add your Application.

- Look through your Friends' Applications to determine what you might want to add.

- If you are serious about having an Application developed, find a development company and get a bid. If nothing else, this is a great exercise in understanding the extent of what may be required. You should also have a clearer understanding of the time and cost to get your Application up and running.

- Comment on the Wall or in discussion Forums about your Application ideas.

QUOTES FROM FACEBOOK USERS

"Applications that update my News Feed are very useful to me. Having blog feeds and viewing what others are doing with Facebook is very cool. I've found a few great applications and groups this way. My Facebook Friends tend to have the same likes I do."

Thom Allen
http:/www.digitalthom.com

"I am using App Tap to search for Facebook Applications because it has the best search results. It guides you to choose the best Applications instead of the popular ones. By voting for Applications in App Tap you can influence others to choose the Applications you like or think are the best. Also, you can easily check other Applications from the same authors, because they are listed on every Application page."

Adam Cox
Independent Facebook Developer
http://apps.facebook.com/ezappbuilder

"Want to discover the newest business Applications on Facebook? Try this strategy. Go to Applications on the left hand side. Click Browse More Applications. Click the Business category. Click Newest to find the most recent business applications. Pick your favorite, click Add Application. Repeat weekly."

Thomas R. Clifford
Award-winning Corporate Filmmaker
http://www.DirectorTom.com

5 Privacy

One of the items on everyone's mind when it comes to Facebook (and other social networking sites) is, "How secure is my information?" This is a very valid concern. Social networking sites allow you to provide a lot of information that could be used in an improper manner by other users, your connections in Facebook, and even Application owners.

It's not uncommon to see news reports of stalkers and child molesters using these sites to gain information about potential victims. The question is, will your information be accessed by those who want to use it for malicious purposes?

Let's go over some of the pros of privacy on Facebook, and how Facebook tries to maintain security for its users in ways other social networking sites have not yet implemented. We'll follow with cons and the privacy issues users of Facebook should be aware of.

1. **Facebook was built to be private.** Facebook originated in the colleges and universities. In the early days, members of Facebook had to be students of a college or university, with a university e-mail address

which Facebook would validate before you could even finish registering. We remember when we couldn't join Facebook because we weren't students.

2. **Only your Friends, and their Friends, are accessible to you.** To view information about any individual on Facebook, you have to be their Friend. There are few exceptions to this rule. For instance, if you invite someone to be a Friend, before that friend even chooses to accept your offer, they can view your full Profile to see who you are. Also, depending on *their* Profile settings, you can see other people's full Profiles if you are on the same Network.

You can also show your Friends only a "limited profile." The limited profile shows Friends a subset of what you would like their "limited profile" Friends to see. Simply click "Profile" in the upper-right corner of Facebook, then click "Edit Settings" below the "Limited Profile" section near the bottom.

Another exception to this rule is your "public profile." On October 21, 2007, Facebook announced they would allow public profiles to be indexed by search engines. Public Profiles display only limited information in order to respect privacy. This is an additional benefit in our opinion, as it is another way to brand yourself online. This feature can be turned off by clicking "Profile" in the upper-right corner of Facebook, then clicking "Edit Settings" next to "Search" on the page that follows. By default, public search users can see your picture, send you a message, Poke you, request to add you as a Friend, and view your list of Friends. Here is an example of a "public profile":

Name   **Jesse Stay**   Send Message
Poke Him!
View Friends
Add to Friends

The default settings for anyone on Facebook are as follows (all of these settings are configurable):

- *Profile*—"All my networks and all my Friends"
- *Status Updates*—"All my networks and all my Friends"

- *"Allow my Friends to subscribe to my Status updates"*—checked
- *Videos Tagged of You*—"All my networks and all my Friends"
- *Photos Tagged of You*—"All my networks and all my Friends"
- *Online Status*—"All my networks and all my Friends"
- *Friends*—"All my networks and all my Friends"
- *Wall*—"All my networks and all my Friends"
- *IM Screen name, Mobile Phone, Land Phone, Current Address, Website*—"All my networks and all my Friends"
- *"Select who can see your contact e-mails" (for each)*—"Friends Only"
- *Posted items, Groups, Marketplace and each Application you install*—"All my networks and all my Friends"

3. **The more information you and your Friends provide, the less likely you are to see advertisements that you don't want to see.** Spam can be defined as unsolicited e-mail or advertisements. If a user is receiving advertisements they want to see, they are less likely to complain. Facebook is a free service, and they have identified advertising as a revenue stream. The advantage to using a social network such as Facebook is that by giving up some of your privacy, you receive more of the advertising you would prefer to receive rather than completely unsolicited sales ads.

From a marketing perspective, this is a gold mine! Never before has a marketer had such specific user information, in such a viral atmosphere. Marketers can detect exactly who you are and have a *much* better idea of things you might be interested in. Because the ads are usually more relevant (but not always), users may be more inclined to share those ads with their Friends.

4. **User information and interests can indicate market trends.** As you get more Friends, Facebook will become a completely new experience for you. We find ourselves going back to News Feeds again and again to see which Groups people are joining, causes people are subscribing to, Friends people are adding, and Events people are attending. By combining all of this information,

it is easy to see what is popular in your circle of Friends. Your circle of Friends becomes your community—a community that gives you a strong idea of popular trends happening in society.

What if you add your competition as a friend? If they accept the friendship (keep in mind they can track you!), you will have a new tool to track what they are doing. You can see which Events they are attending, Groups they belong to, people they are developing relationships with, and from all that you may even be able to tell *how* they do what they do. This is extremely valuable information!

5. **All this information can be available to applications *you* develop!** As a business, you have access to a plethora of information[31] regarding individuals that install any software you write on the Facebook platform. You can see how this can be an invaluable tool for you to use to establish your own brand identity on Facebook while gathering extremely valuable demographics about the individuals that are interested in your brand. Such demographics could also be used to build your brand outside of Facebook.

6. **Application data is protected.** We can't talk about how much information Application owners have access to without mentioning that the information they have access to is protected. Although they do have access to this information, the users of Facebook themselves are also protected.

Application developers have access to most of the data in a user's profile, and most of the data in a user's Friends' Profiles. While this information is accessible, the terms of use for a developer on Facebook prohibit the storing of most of this information without the user's explicit permission.

If a developer violates this clause and it is discovered, Facebook can (and has), without notice, disable the developer's profile, kill the Application, and prohibit further use of Facebook. This isn't foolproof, but Facebook does take measures to protect your privacy. The exact limits are stated in the Developer section.

Per the Developer Terms of Use, you may not cache any user data for more than 24 hours, with the exception of information that is explicitly "storable indefinitely." Only the following parameters/values

---

31. http://developers.facebook.com/documentation.php?v=1.0&doc=misc.

are storable indefinitely; all other information must be requested from Facebook each time:

uid—User ID

nid—Primary network ID

eid—Event ID

gid—Group ID

pid—Photo ID

aid—Photo album ID

notes_count—Total number of Notes written by the user

profile_update_time—Time that the user's profile was last updated

The storable IDs enable you to keep unique identifiers for Facebook elements that correspond to data gathered by your Application(s). For instance, if you collect information about a user's musical tastes, you could associate that data with a user's Facebook UID.

However, note that you cannot store any relations between these IDs, such as whether a user is attending an Event. The only exception is the user-to-network relation.

In summary, an Application developer may only store the IDs of the objects you are tracking, and any data you want to collect surrounding those ids must be obtained through corresponding Facebook platform API calls. This makes it very difficult for people to use the information for the wrong purposes.

Now let's talk about the cons. You'll see some items listed as cons that are also pros above—this is intentional. Every piece of information shared by a user means two things: first, the user is giving up some of their privacy, but second, they can have a better user experience.Such shared information also provides an additional revenue opportunity for businesses.

1. **Your information, and your Friends' information, is available to any Application you install.** Developers are fully aware of the power the Facebook platform brings to any business willing to put to use its incredible network of information. Earlier in the chapter

we mention a list of the information developers are allowed to store legally, i.e., without the user's permission. This does not mean the developer won't store more information. Most of the information you see on your Profile and your Friends' Profiles can be retrieved by a Facebook Application, then stored on the servers where that Application is hosted.

Of course, if the owners of that Application are caught, they risk being banned from Facebook, but this does not stop all Applications developers from doing so. The Facebook developer documentation[32] itemizes all of the information a Facebook Application can technically retrieve. While not approved by Facebook, the capability to store and archive that data is also possible. The developer documentation is quite technical, but it can give you an understanding of what data developers have access to.

Not to scare you further, but you should know your data is accessible to an Application that your Friend has loaded, even if *you* haven't loaded the Application. This means that your data could be sent to the owner of an Application that a Friend added, even if *you have not* added the Application.

2. **Any Application you add, any Wall conversation or comment, and any link you post are also shared with your Friends via their News Feed.** We previously defined this as a pro, but we also want to remind you to always take caution in what you write on your Friends Walls, what links you post, what Status updates you send, what pictures you post—basically anything you do on Facebook. Most of your interactions on Facebook can be displayed in your Friends' News Feed and therefore they, too, can see what you are saying. If there is something you don't want all of your Friends to see, we suggest you send a personal e-mail to the individual.

One example of this was when Jesse's brother (Luke) got engaged. He was trying to keep it secret until the right time to tell friends and family. Jesse happened to find out from his mother and, without thinking, tried to confirm it on Luke's Facebook profile Wall. Both Luke and his fiancé were soon getting inquiries about the status of their relationship! It is a good idea to think twice before posting something to Facebook.

---

32. http://tinyurl.com/2e7h55.

As we mentioned earlier in the chapter, this can all be configured in your preferences; if there is something you don't want your Friends to see, you should turn it off in your preferences. Some items, however (e.g., Wall posts), just can't be hidden from your Facebook Friends. *Think twice* before hitting that submit button.

3. **Facebook "Beacon" can reveal items you purchase that you may not want your Friends to know you bought.** Beacon is a service which allows retailers to store a cookie on your computer when you purchase from them online. That cookie can be read by Facebook, and Facebook can share the information with your Friends. This is a neat feature, as it allows us to see what our Friends are purchasing and gets us asking them what they think about it. We make purchasing decisions considering what our Friends buy, don't you? It is also great for retailers because, as they get more exposure on Facebook, more people might want to buy the item when they see *their* Friends have purchased it from the retailer.

However, it is easy to see the privacy issues at stake. As we were writing this book, Beacon was a huge issue in the news. It was released shortly before Christmas 2006, and became a concern when users started complaining that Christmas they were buying appeared in the News Feed of Friends (and family) they were buying for!

The issue became such a concern that MoveOn.org issued a statement against the new Facebook advertising system. The main concern was that the new system had no "opt-in" feature. You could opt-out of receiving solicitation from individual advertisers (after the fact) via the privacy settings, but most people wouldn't know this information was sent to their Friends. Facebook has since partially rectified the problem by allowing a user to opt-out of Beacon. They have also required users to agree to the ads appearing on their Friends' News Feeds before the ads actually appear.

Again, *after* you make the purchase you can turn off Beacon's notices by going to your Privacy Settings Page (upper-right corner in Facebook) and clicking "External Websites." Within that section you may also completely turn off Beacon by checking "Don't allow any websites to send stories to my profile."

Privacy is, and will be, a hot topic in Facebook. You'll see it mentioned on bleeding edge blogs as well as in traditional big newspapers. To conclude this chapter we'll point you to an excellent article from Internet Duct Tape, "How to use Facebook without Losing Your Job Over It,"[33] as well as a scary look at Facebook privacy issues in a popular video.[34]

ACTION ITEMS

- Look at your News Feed page to see what info you see by default, then determine what you are comfortable showing your Friends.

- Go into the Privacy Page and adjust your settings as appropriate.

- Remove any Application that isn't necessary or doesn't add value to your strategy, realizing that Application owners have significant access to your profile (regardless of your privacy settings).

- See if you can spot a Friend in your News Feed that has purchased from an advertiser using Facebook's Beacon.

- Share your Privacy questions and concerns on the "I'm on Facebook—Now What???" Facebook Page at http://www.facebook.com/profile.php?id=6816644117.

- Sign up for a MySpace and a LinkedIn account and compare the privacy features between those two and Facebook.

---

33. http://tinyurl.com/2v7sep.
34. http://albumoftheday.com/facebook.

QUOTES FROM FACEBOOK USERS

"Privacy on Facebook is a huge issue. Facebook's intellectual property clauses can be summed up as "We have a perpetual license to your stuff."

Christopher S. Penn
CTO, The Student Loan Network
http://www.FinancialAidPodcast.com

"Careful use of the settings can block people who might potentially be 'undesirable.' For example, to expand my business network, I allow requests from people who either give a polite reason to be connected or whom I might know by reputation. I place them on 'limited profile' where they cannot see my private photo albums."

Jack Yan
CEO, Jack Yan & Associates
http://www.jackyan.com
Wellington, New Zealand

"Facebook Marketplace is really quite important. It's like a mini eBay without the bidding. People put everything from jobs in your area, to a brand new TV that they bought that is too big for their house, and they're selling it for a discounted price. People find roommates, or just a person who will buy their 91 Air Jordans from them. I might have found a job using Marketplace."

Dorothy Taffet
UCONN

Chapter

6 Your Facebook Strategy

Jesse is the oldest of six children and still has teenage sisters. When his baby sister turned seventeen, living on the other side of the U.S., he decided it was time to find a way to keep an eye on her. He talked to his younger brother who suggested Facebook as the "in" thing among younger kids.

Jesse joined and quickly found what his sister's Friends were saying back and forth, pictures of the boys she was hanging out with... now he could be a real older brother and watch out for her! Soon he found he could do way more than just see what boys his sister was hanging out with—he began finding old elementary school buddies. He found Facebook to be a great distribution channel for his blog posts. He found it to be a great way to message people and get their attention in a way that he couldn't with e-mail. He began networking like he never had before. He was using Facebook as a tool, not just a means of recreation.

As the title of this book indicates, many people get on Facebook and wonder, "What am I supposed to do next?" What is it that people do that keeps them so involved in Facebook? We hear these questions often as we consult and talk to others about Facebook. If it weren't for our curiosity to see what others were doing, we would have the same questions! In this chapter we hope to clarify some of what we found, and also give you a routine so you can see how Facebook can be such a useful tool for you.

How Much Time Should I Spend on Facebook?

That's a question we can't answer for you. How do you see Facebook being useful to you? Find the parts of Facebook that will simplify your life, and spend some time putting them to use! Do you want to use it as a networking tool? Spend time Social Network Optimizing to ensure you are seen by the people you want to connect with. Do you want to stay in touch with old friends? Then spend time finding those old friends, login to see when their birthdays are—wish them a happy birthday on their Wall, reach out to them.

Prioritize your needs and decide if you can get more done using Facebook than other tools can provide. We suggest making a plan and trying it out for a short time to see how it works. For some, Facebook is a way of living—live it and experience it—and if it isn't working for you, perhaps you need to tweak your plan. Here are some things you could do, grouped by the different types of people that use Facebook today:

> **TIP** To help ensure you optimize your time on Facebook, determine in advance what your Facebook goals are.

Student

- *Find classmates*—let's say you met someone in one of your classes that you want to study with. Perhaps you're having a difficult time with a particular subject, but you know a classmate who is more knowledgeable in that subject. Perhaps you met a cute guy or girl you want to ask out on a date. With Facebook, all you need to know is their name, and a quick search can lead you to their Profile.

Jesse likes to check for names of classmates he went to school with. He went to elementary school in Jakarta, Indonesia. He doesn't get to talk to many of his friends anymore, but he knew some really cool people there. Guess what? He found the elementary school's Facebook Group, JIS, and posted some questions in the Forums. He was quickly hearing back from multiple classmates, including the fifth grade teacher who helped inspire him to learn about computers, Mr. Reinsmoen. Now, he is again connected to many of those classmates and teachers!

TIP Look for old classmates, even back through elementary school.

- *Communicate with your professor*—we know of several university professors who use Facebook. If your professor uses Facebook (look them up!), drop them a message on their Wall and let them know you appreciated their last lecture. Have a question from class? Send them a Facebook message! Encourage them to use the Groups features of Facebook and then participate in Forums for your class Group. What if they don't use Facebook? Purchase them a copy of this book and encourage them to use Facebook! Facebook can be an excellent way for professors to stay in touch with their students.

- *Collaborate with classmates*—find your class Group. Don't see one? Create one and invite all your classmates to join. Create a topic for each lecture—discuss it and learn from your classmates! Send your classmates questions via your mobile phone through Facebook's mobile messaging service during (just don't get caught!) or after the lecture. Ask a question in your Facebook Status and see if any of your Friends know the answer. Depending on your privacy settings, keep in mind that what you do may be visible to your professor, so certainly don't do anything on Facebook that your professor might object to!

An Application you might want to consider is Class Talk, which allows you to find and collaborate with other students in your class.

- *Study for a test*—there are some great study tools on Facebook. One Application to search for is Share Homework, which allows you to share and collaborate on homework with your classmates.

Another great Application is Class Point. Class Point loads your classes and lets you collaborate with other students in those classes. The Cheap Textbooks Application lets you compare text book prices, then chooses a text book with the lowest price. The Tutor Application helps you find those who provide tutoring at your school. If you search around, you'll find what you need to get all your studying needs taken care of.

- *Learn about a professor*—one useful Application you might want to consider is the Rate Teachers Application. This allows you to anonymously list your teachers and then share with other class-mates how those teachers rate. This can be especially useful when selecting your teachers or professors for the next year. School administrators should pay attention to this as well, as it could show which teachers are performing well.

Employee

- *Collaborate with other employees*—Facebook can be a useful tool to keep other employees updated on what you're doing. The Status updates are a great, public way to inform people of your day-to-day activities. Private Groups can be organized where your company can have a Forum, a Wall, Notes, photos and more.

> **TIP** Create a Facebook badge by clicking "profile", then "Create a Profile Badge" at the bottom.

One example is a Group set up by Jesse's former employer. The Group is private, so we don't know all the details, but it is a novel way to give a "hint" to the community that their Group was working on something big while also establishing a place where they could build community among their employees. Jesse saw employees shoot Wall posts to one another, and has communicated with their CEO via Facebook e-mail. There are many possibilities for making Facebook bring efficiencies to your job.

- *Position yourself*—let's face it, office politics are a fact of life. Knowing what your coworkers are doing can help you know what you can do better in order to get that big raise or promotion, or show your employer that you are worth what they are paying you. While we don't encourage bragging, the Facebook Status messages and Wall posts on prospective customer Profiles can be a way to show your coworkers that you are on top of things. If anything, this keeps the competitive spirit flowing in the work place.

- *Learn from others in your field*—be sure to try and emulate people whom you admire. Observing the things smart and successful people are doing can open an entirely new world to you. The News Feed is great for this. Send a Facebook e-mail to individuals highlighted in the feed and, when people respond, nurture individual relationships.

TIP Create an invite-only Group for your department.

- *Keep track of what your coworkers are doing*—if you need to be sure you're on par with a Group project, use Facebook. Share Notes with each other. Post images, diagrams and photos with each other via Facebook Photos. Keep your status updated via Facebook Status. As long as the information is as private as the privacy settings allow, Facebook can be a great tool for intra-company communications.

- *Share documentation*—Facebook's Notes, Posted Items, and Photos are excellent ways to share and collaborate in Facebook. Specify who you want to share these with, i.e., make them public, or share with only your Friends, or with only certain coworkers.

Business Owner

- *Keep track of your employees*—we're not suggesting you "spy" on your employees, but we are suggesting employers allow and encourage Facebook use in the workplace. Then add all your employees as Friends. By doing so, not only will you be able to collaborate with your employees, you may also be able to identify issues such as miscommunication or low productivity.

- *Stay up with the competition*—we suggested earlier that you add your competition as Friends. As long as you are aware they can see what you are doing, this might even the game in many ways. It may allow you to keep up with what they are doing and even getting hints on their strategies. Facebook can also be a great way to see potential *new* competitors. Search for key terms relative to what you do on Facebook, and other startups and potential competitors of yours may show up on your radar.

- *Attract potential customers*—ensure you have information on your Profile that will allow others to find you. When they search for people with particular skills, or items they want to purchase, they are likely to come across your profile and contact you. Just as Jesse was writing this, a person he didn't know contacted him, asking for some help to get a Facebook Application working. A good portion of Jesse's clients actually come directly through Facebook.

Facebook Pages are another great way to attract potential customers. When you create a Page for your brand, your users are given one more venue to show their support for your brand. They can subscribe as Fans of your brand, and *their* Friends will see the support they give you. This can spread your brand virally.

TIP Look up "I'm on Facebook—Now What???" on Facebook. There you'll find the Page for this book.

Also, try writing a Facebook Application for your brand. It doesn't have to be something your company does online, but it can be something that highlights your brand and generates buzz. Write a contest Application and encourage the users of the Application to do something. If they do, they win one of your products. Partner with other Application developers to associate your brand with their Applications. Application developers on Facebook are always looking for ways to monetize their Applications, so it might be easier than you think.

- *Virally spread your brand*—create social ads on Facebook. These are ads that appear with the picture of someone who clicked on your ad, associating them with your brand to their Friends. Look into Facebook Beacon—when users shop on your non-Facebook website, you can have their purchases appear in Facebook to their Friends, encouraging them to click over to your website. Write viral Applications to spread your brand. Create Groups and Pages for your brand, and encourage the users in those Groups to share with their Friends on Facebook.

- *Organize your team*—we mentioned earlier the company that created an internal, private Group on Facebook to organize thoughts and ideas on a particular project. Facebook Groups are excellent tools to get the teams within your company to work together and collaborate. Use Facebook Events to remind employees of upcoming due dates or project deadlines. There are many ways to accomplish this collaborative communication.

Mom or Dad

- *Keep track of your children*—Jesse shares the story of keeping an eye on his sister. Recently, he noticed his aunts and uncles (in their 40s to 60s) are starting to join Facebook. We applaud them for this—they are discovering a new world their kids are associated with. It's always funny to see Wall posts of Friends saying they're not quite sure what to think about their mom or dad being on Facebook, but believe us, as parents, this is one of the best things you can do to keep track of your children.

TIP Add your kids and other relatives as friends.

- *Unify your family*—Jesse's family has created a Facebook Group just for themselves. They post family photos, have discussions, share stories, and some times even make fun of each other. It has built more unity within the family. Every so often Jesse will send a Facebook "gift" to family members, those little $1 graphics you can buy and send to others that show up on their Wall. They get birthday reminders and wish one another happy birthday on their Walls. All these tools have brought them closer as a family.

- *Find your ancestors*—We're Related, by FamilyLink.com, is a fantastic Application we recommend to any family on Facebook. They went from 0 to 1.5 million users in just a few months, making it one of the most popular Applications on Facebook. With We're Related, you can link your Facebook Friends that are related to you and see *how* they are related to you. It will try to detect other Friends that might be relatives based on information they submitted. It provides a means to track birthdays, Status messages and

Events happening among all your family members, as well as have your own family Forums in which you can discuss family matters with each other.

- *Find the latest news and information to help your family*—do you subscribe to a lot of RSS feeds? The Feedheads Application may be for you. Feedheads tracks all of the Favorites that your Friends have shared in Google Reader and NewsGator, then shares the most popular ones with you so you can be in synch with the latest and greatest news and information. If a lot of your Friends on Facebook are moms and dads, this could be an excellent way to get the latest information on mom and dad issues.

Example Day in Facebook

In his own words, here are some of the things Jesse does daily on Facebook:

1. **I love searching for new Friends.** I have set the rule that I only add Friends that I know or have associated with directly in some fashion or another, or those who are directly interested in me or what I do. This makes my Friends list more powerful. A few exceptions include Friends I'm trying to get to know better and those for whom I'm trying to build a strategy for getting on their radar.

   Generally, I find most of my Friends by just watching my News Feed and seeing which Friends my own Friends are adding. Chances are most of the Friends you know have had some contact with your other Friends. I do, however, occasionally search for former classmates, coworkers and friends I grew up with. There are some great search tools, including an advanced search (click on the search text above the search box) which you can use to for this purpose. You can also use the Friend Finder[35] in Facebook to find old friends—this can be accessed through the Friend Finder link on the right side of your Friends page. I use this occasionally to find those that graduated at or around the same time I did from my high school and college.

---

35. https://register.facebook.com/findfriends.php.

2. **I'm constantly working on some sort of Facebook Page for one of my brands.** I am currently building one for this book, I have one for SocialOptimize.com, my consulting company, and I'm working one more.

3. **I participate in various Facebook Groups.** I have several from previous high schools, colleges and employers I frequent to get in touch with old friends and network further. I also use Groups to advertise new Applications I am working on.

4. **I write Facebook Applications.** I am constantly testing my Applications' new features, checking their statistics and new users' status, and participating in the discussion boards and Walls for each of the Applications I develop.

5. **I check my News Feed very often.** This is where I find out what my friends, clients, coworkers and others are doing on a daily basis. It's an invaluable tool for keeping myself informed of their interests, finding new contacts, and finding opportunities to be of assistance.

6. **I use Facebook Mobile to upload photos of Events I am participating in.** I often take pictures with my iPhone, and with a simple MMS message to mobile@facebook.com, it automatically posts the pictures to my profile for others to see, tag themselves in, and share with others. You can tag yourself or any of your friends on any picture in Facebook by clicking "Tag this Photo", clicking on the person in the picture to whom you wish to attach a name, then selecting or typing the name of that person.

7. **I use Facebook to update my Status in real-time.** you can always tell what I'm doing and where I am, because I have Twitter send all updates of what I am doing and where I am directly to Facebook. You can also do this with Facebook Mobile, which is connected with most providers except T-Mobile.

8. **I upload photos.** I use a plug-in for Picasa (and iPhoto) that interfaces directly with Facebook to upload my photos. It also serves as a secondary archive for other photos I may not want to upload into Facebook just yet. The iPhoto plug-in even lets me tag those in the photo and link them with my Facebook Friends!

9. **I syndicate my blog.** You can give Facebook Notes an RSS feed to load. Every time you post a new blog feed, Facebook Notes will update and let your Friends know that you have posted a new item to your blog.

We can go on and on, but you get the point. There are plenty of useful things to do in Facebook. Facebook is more than just a playground—it is a tool that all of us can use to make our lives more productive and help us survive in this world of high-tech networking and fast-moving information.

ACTION ITEMS

- Determine your purpose and goals for using Facebook.

- List activities that you should do to meet those goals (Groups to join, Applications to add, Events to create, etc.).

- Develop a regular schedule of maintenance tasks, especially considering the value of pinging your Friends regularly.

- Evaluate your return (responses, etc.) to ensure you get value out of your account and time invested.

- Record how you currently spend time in Facebook, then modify your schedule and Facebook activities to be more productive.

- Invite three new people to Facebook that were not previously members.

- Add your children as Friends!

QUOTES FROM FACEBOOK USERS

"I use Facebook to promote professional groups I am involved in and drive membership numbers. I link blog posts about the association and post association events to virally marketing the association. By inviting colleagues that are currently a member of the organization, I open the door for them to introduce the group to their non-member colleagues and in turn spread information and good will about the organization and member benefits."

Barbara Safani
President
www.CareerSolvers.com

"Develop a specific plan for connecting with potential strategic partners, co-authors, distributors for your products and/or services, and guest bloggers for your own blog. Also, be SMART[1] about your Facebook goals. You might want to word your goal this way: "Establish three new relationships on Facebook with potential strategic business partners within the next six months."

Susan Guarneri
Career Assessment Goddess
http://www.AssessmentGoddess.com

1. http://blog.careergoddess.com/blog/2008/01/smart-goals-for.html.

7 Facebook for Business(es)

Let's start this chapter with **Rule #1: Etiquette.** Of course this applies to any aspect of Facebook (not just for this business chapter) and any other social network or social experience. Be very careful when trying to promote yourself or your company. Do everything you can to *not* cross the lines of Internet etiquette, or all of your work might backfire on you—and your brand can become smeared in ways you never wanted to imagine.

Just what does etiquette in Facebook mean? In general, it's more effective to be a contributor to the community rather than pitch (or advertise). For instance, how can you add value to someone, as they use Facebook, so they consider you a subject matter expert? Vincent Wright, founder of MyLinkedInPowerForum (MLPF),[36] reminds his 8,000 Yahoo! Group list members of this in a regular message:

> "While it is the full intention of MLPF to help each of its members to grow their businesses and enhance their careers via stronger networking, MLPF is a discussion group. It is not an advertising board. Going forward, the

---

36. http://tinyurl.com/3ax9ps.

message section will be reserved for discussion, for conversation ONLY[37].... turn it into a discussion."[38]

This is great advice for businesses who want to promote themselves in Facebook. Pages was introduced in November of 2007, allowing a profile for a non-person entity. Before Pages was introduced, Facebook only allowed personal Profiles to be created. Allowing non-person Profiles meant that "businesses, bands, celebrities and more"[39] could have a place to gather Friends, create Events, have a Wall and collect other communication (videos, pictures, etc.).

As you grow your community you'll have one more way to get information out about news and Events. Again, how can you add value to your community? Instead of having laser focus on your specific product or offering, consider delivering content that is relevant and useful to your target market, even if it's not specifically promoting your offering. As you become a thought-leader in the space, you'll find you have more people interested in your community and your message, even if they weren't initially interested.

Obviously, aside from contributing to a community you will also want to promote your product or service. In other words, you don't have to come across as a neutral content provider, but community members want to know that you are honest, sincere and interested in their needs. How do you do both?

There are many businesses that are working to develop greater interaction and a strong presence on Facebook, including non-profits, for-profits, government, etc. Enter the names of your competition in the search box to see if they are there. What comes up? For example, if we worked at Jobster we would check to see what Monster and Career-Builder are doing. If you do a search on these and go through the first few pages of results, you might find it interesting that some Groups are corporate-sponsored while others were created by Fans.

To see the good, the bad and the ugly of what Fans can create, simply search for a current politician. You will find support Groups as well as

---

37. http://tech.groups.yahoo.com/group/MyLinkedinPowerForum/message/31826.
38. http://tech.groups.yahoo.com/group/MyLinkedinPowerForum/message/31821.
39. http://blog.facebook.com/blog.php?post=6972252130.

"burn in hell," or worse. It makes sense that some organizations, whether they are your company or a politician's team, work to make the negative Groups less significant, even if it means having your Fans create support Groups. But let's try and focus on the good stuff for now.

TIP If you have a business, create a "Page".

When we do a search for Project Manager the very first hit is a Page for EZ Project Manager, by Zen Solutions. The other nine hits on that first page of results are all people, but it sure is interesting that a company page is at the top of the list. More interesting is that the page only has three Fans... we wonder what would happen with the search results if another page with more Fans came along?

Page:	**EZ Project Manager**
Type:	Technology Product / Service
Matches:	Name

When looking at Groups or Applications on Facebook, there are certain things that are going to lend credibility. One obvious measure is the adoption rate. Facebook usually tells you how many total members are using an Application, or are in a Group, as well as the daily users and the usage percentage of your Network. While the Adoption rate is not a foolproof measurement, it does seem to make that Group, Page or Application more (or less) popular, and therefore more (or less) trust-worthy.

TIP If you manage a Group, be careful to not e-mail your group members too frequently.

What can you do to increase the number of adopters to a Group, Page or Application? There's no substitute for savvy marketing, and of course viral marketing and sheer luck have a lot to do with it. We would argue that Jobster's Group would have just a few hundred members except for the fact that they were able to:

1. **Get good press.** If you Google "Jobster Facebook" (without the quotes) you'll see a number of leading news sites and blogs talking about the Jobster/Facebook relationship—something that clearly raised the awareness of Jobster in general, perhaps driving new users to Jobster *and* Facebook.

2. **Use your own community.** Jobster already had a community of users and a way to communicate with them. You can see various mentions of Facebook on the Jobster blog, but the key is in this e-mail that went out to all Jobster users:

   > Hey there,
   >
   > I usually send our users a "Jobster tips and tricks" Note every 2 weeks but with this breaking news, I just couldn't wait to tell you...
   >
   > Jobster just launched our new Application on Facebook. Check it out at http://apps.facebook.com/jobster and sign up for employer talent networks.
   >
   > Learn more details on our blog at http://jobster.blogs.com.[40]

   The message went out to their own users, with a link and invitation to the Application, and a link for more information at their blog. If you have an e-mail list, community of users, etc. make sure you push your news out to them.

3. **Partner with Facebook.** Okay, this is kind of tongue-in-cheek, as it's probably next to impossible to be the next legitimate Facebook partner. But the simple fact that they have this relationship surely drove thousands of users to their Group and Application.

careercenter	Group:	Career Center: meet your future
	Network:	Global
	Size:	27,400 members
	Type:	Sponsored
	New:	3 Board Topics
	Matches:	Description

---

40. Message sent to Jason, as a Jobster user, on July 30, 2007 from former Jobster CEO Jason Goldberg.

Check out what you see when you do a search for Ernst & Young:

	Group:	**Ernst & Young Careers**
	Network:	Global
	Size:	12,089 members
	Type:	Sponsored
	New:	44 More Members, 4 Board Topics, 13 Wall Posts
	Matches:	Name

You can see that Ernst & Young has less than one half the members of Jobster's Career Center (with over 20,000), but it looks like it's growing more and has more activity. Even at half the size of Jobster, we're guessing Ernst & Young is stronger because its 12,089 members are likely interested in employment with Ernst & Young, with degrees and career ambitions that match what Ernst & Young offers. Jobster's members, on the other hand, are probably interested in all kinds of careers, from all kinds of employers. The diversity is good, but accounting and information recruiters are probably more interested in Ernst & Young's members than Jobster's members.

Another way to measure credibility is the brand name, or the supporting website(s) behind the Group or Application. For example, the Wall Street Journal Group only has 288 members right now, which isn't much (it's nothing compared to the millions that are in other Groups), but we all know and trust the Wall Street Journal as a legitimate company, don't we?

As you develop your company strategy on Facebook (and other social networks, for that matter), keep in mind it's probably better to have a strong, aggressive strategy that builds a large community than a somewhat lonely and limited community. I'm much more impressed that Fans of MarketingProfs has over six hundred members in their Group compared to WSJ's almost three hundred members. What if you only get three members? What impression will that give to prospects, or even current customers, if your community strategy is a perceived failure?

A strong social strategy for your business is critical to staying on top of the game and ensuring your brand continues to stay at the forefront of everyone's mind. The return a good Facebook strategy can give you is well worth the money invested (usually very little to nothing!).

ACTION ITEMS

- Find businesses in competitive or complementary industries and analyze their strategies.

- Find businesses completely outside of your space and begin to develop a "best practices" list that you can work towards duplicating.

- Develop a plan for your business to implement particularly useful Applications, Pages, Groups, etc.

- Create a Facebook Page for your business.

- Create a Facebook Group for your department—make it private so only members of your department can access the Group.

- Contact a social networking firm to discuss further ways to bring a Facebook strategy into your own business.

QUOTE FROM A FACEBOOK USER

"Our Lucire Group, which is accessible to anyone, has proven to be a good complement to our email newsletters, RSS feeds and general online marketing. How can you not have one these days? To get people surfing into it, we actually post updates of new articles there first. Given that our readers are people who either read our fashion magazine or want to be a step ahead of fashion, our Group provides them with some of the immediacy they expect."

Jack Yan
CEO, Jack Yan & Associates
http://www.jackyan.com
Wellington, New Zealand

8 Facebook No-No's

In 2007, a blogger who goes by the name Jon Swift (taken as a tribute to the Swift Boat veterans) was banned from Facebook for allegedly not using his real name in his Profile. From his blog:[41]

> Earlier this week I logged into Facebook and discovered that without warning my account had been deleted. According to Facebook, I am a fake, a charlatan, a nonperson and all of my more than 200 Facebook Friends are the victims of a cruel hoax. My crime? Violating Facebook's Terms of Use by not using my "real name."

Swift had been banned, shunned by Facebook per its Terms of Use, despite the fact he goes by Jon Swift. Swift was bitten by a small clause in Facebook's Terms of Use that says, "In consideration of your use of the Site, you agree to (a) provide accurate, current and complete information about you as may be prompted by any registration forms on the Site ('Registration Data')..." In addition, he violated another clause saying one agrees to not use the site or service to "impersonate any person or entity, or falsely state or otherwise misrepresent yourself, your age or

41. http://tinyurl.com/2cmxra.

your affiliation with any person or entity..."[42] Swift, while simply trying to protect his online anonymity, became victim to the exact thing Facebook was trying to protect—personal privacy.

After some prodding by a large Group devoted to restoring his account on Facebook, and the support of many bloggers, Jon Swift's account was restored, with the following note from Facebook:[43]

> Upon further review, we have decided to reactivate your account. Our Terms of Use, to which all users agree when they first sign up for the site, stipulate that you must not "impersonate any person or entity, or falsely state or otherwise misrepresent yourself, your age or your affiliation with any person or entity."

> However, since others on the site seem to know you by this name, and since you don't appear to be using the name to impersonate or to hide your identity, we have determined that you are not violating these Terms. We apologize for any inconvenience this has caused. Please let me know if you have further questions or concerns.

> Thanks for your understanding...

Swift had become a very vocal target towards pseudonym accounts on Facebook, but as he points out, there are many more with fictitious names, including "Jesus Christ." His own pseudonym, "Jon Swift," is common on Facebook. This just goes to show that there are many "no-no's," both legally and socially that one must be aware of when using Facebook.

Another example was Harry Joiner, the Marketing Headhunter.[44] Joiner, after reading Robert Scoble's blog entry about using Facebook as a Rolodex,[45] decided to invite all 4,200 of his Gmail contacts to Facebook.[46] All he did was use tools made available to him by Facebook, and acted in a manner that seemed acceptable by Facebook. Apparently, it wasn't.

---

42. http://www.facebook.com/terms.php.
43. http://tinyurl.com/2cmxra.
44. http://www.marketingheadhunter.com.
45. http://www.recruitingbloggers.com/rbs/2007/11/harry-joiner-re.html.
46. http://www.recruitingbloggers.com/rbs/2007/08/scoble-scorns-f.html.

They interpreted this as spam and quickly terminated Joiner's account. It seems Facebook had interpreted Joiner's use of invites under a clause in their Terms of Use stating that the site was not to be used to "...upload, post, transmit, share or otherwise make available any unsolicited or unauthorized advertising, solicitations, promotional materials, 'junk mail', 'spam', 'chain letters', 'pyramid schemes', or any other form of solicitation..."

All Harry did was use the tools on the site, and his account was terminated. After a very vocal battle and even a "do not try this at home" warning from Robert Scoble himself, Facebook reinstated Joiner's account with the following letter:

> Your account was disabled because you took repeated actions that could be construed as spam.
>
> For instance, it is a violation of Facebook's Terms of Use to repeatedly send the same message or to make the same post. Facebook prides itself in protecting users from spam, and we take this standard very seriously.
>
> However, after reviewing your situation, we have reactivated your account, and you should now be able to login. Please refrain from sending the same message or repeating the same post, as further violations of our Terms will result in your account being permanently disabled.
>
> Please also be aware that when a warning message appears on your home page, it will generally be displayed for 24 hours. It can be displayed for longer, however, if you continue to perform these actions. We appreciate your cooperation going forward.
>
> Thanks for your understanding...

Swift and Joiner were lucky. Because of their vocal platforms, they were able to argue their position and become reinstated to Facebook. There are many more stories, however, of people who were not so fortunate and have not been able to get their accounts reinstated. Let's go over some of the highlights of Facebook's Terms of Use so that you can understand what to beware of.

Facebook's Terms of Use[47]

It is worth noting that Facebook's Terms of Use leave little room for argument. Whether you are a registered member or not, you agree to abide by their Terms of Use just by visiting the Facebook Profile (this is pretty common in website Terms of Use agreements). Also, any damages sought cannot exceed that paid by the user (which is usually nothing), with $1,000 maximum in damages. All damages are to be sought after through arbitration, not the courts. This means Facebook definitely has the upper hand if their Terms of Use are deemed to be fair and reasonable. One could argue the legalities and whether this could be admitted in court, but those are the rules they have in place.

Below are some noteworthy rules to abide by, per the Facebook Terms of Use (keep in mind that we list only a few here). We suggest you spend more time checking them in depth by clicking the link "Terms" at the bottom of any Facebook Page:

- Per the terms, "This Site is intended solely for users who are thirteen (13) years of age or older, and users of the Site under 18 who are currently in high school or college. Any registration by, use of or access to the Site by anyone under 13, or by anyone who is under 18 and not in high school or college, is unauthorized, unlicensed and in violation of these Terms of Use."—meaning, if you are under 18 and not in college or high school, you are not supposed to sign up in Facebook and your site will be removed if discovered.

- You must provide accurate and complete information, e.g., use your *real* name.

- You must maintain the security of your password and identification.

- You must keep your registration information data up-to-date.

- You may not violate the copyrights of third parties.

- You may not harvest e-mails for spam.

- You "[may not] use automated scripts to collect information from or otherwise interact with the Service or the Site;"

---

47. http://www.facebook.com/terms.php.

- You "[may not] upload, post, transmit, share, store or otherwise make available any content that [Facebook deems] to be harmful, threatening, unlawful, defamatory, infringing, abusive, inflammatory, harassing, vulgar, obscene, fraudulent, invasive of privacy or publicity rights, hateful, or racially, ethnically or otherwise objectionable;"

- You may not post videos, images, or content not belonging to you or your Friends.

- You may not have more than one account or sign up for an account on behalf of someone other than yourself (or Group or entity).

- You may not publicly make available any private information about other individuals.

- You may not intimidate or harass others using Facebook.

- Facebook lists, in large print, the following regarding Facebook Pages, so one should consider this when entering information on a Facebook Page:

"FACEBOOK DOES NOT PRE-SCREEN OR APPROVE FACEBOOK PAGES, AND CANNOT GUARANTEE THAT A FACEBOOK PAGE WAS ACTUALLY CREATED AND IS BEING OPERATED BY THE INDIVIDUAL OR ENTITY THAT IS THE SUBJECT OF A FACEBOOK PAGE. NOR IS FACEBOOK RESPONSIBLE FOR THE CONTENT OF ANY FACEBOOK PAGE, OR ANY TRANSACTIONS ENTERED INTO OR OTHER ACTIONS TAKEN ON OR IN CONNECTION WITH ANY FACEBOOK PAGE, INCLUDING HOW THE OWNER OF THE FACEBOOK PAGE COLLECTS, HANDLES, USES AND / OR SHARES ANY PERSONAL INFORMATION IT MAY COLLECT FROM USERS (PLEASE REVIEW THE FACEBOOK PRIVACY POLICY IF YOU HAVE ANY QUESTIONS OR CONCERNS REGARDING THE USE OR SHARING OF YOUR PERSONAL INFORMATION). YOU SHOULD BE CAREFUL BEFORE PROVIDING ANY PERSONAL INFORMATION TO OR ENTERING INTO ANY TRANSACTION IN CONNECTION WITH A FACEBOOK PAGE."

If this is profoundly interesting to you, you may want to check out these additional resources (and terms):

- Facebook Pages Terms
  http://www.facebook.com/terms_pages.php

- Terms of Sale for items purchased on Facebook
  http://www.facebook.com/termsofsale.php

- Code of Conduct
  http://www.facebook.com/codeofconduct.php

- Report Copyright infringement to
  http://www.facebook.com/copyright.php

- Facebook Marketplace Guidelines
  http://www.facebook.com/marketplace/guidelines.php

- Facebook Developer Terms of Use
  http://developers.facebook.com/terms.php

- Facebook Platform Application Guidelines
  http://developers.facebook.com/guidelines.php

Moral and Social No-No's

In 2007, Jasmine Kalimullah and Hannah Simmons started a Group on Facebook called "30 Reasons Girls Should Call it a Night." They allowed anyone to join and, through the Group, users posted thousands (4,746 at the time of this writing) of photos of drunken girls, many passed out, for the world to see. Some of the photos showed girls in embarrassing situations, some half-dressed. None of the pictures leave a good first impression for any of these girls. The founders of the Group removed some of the more embarrassing photos and those that violated Facebook terms, but still, this Group has raised many questions as to what is and isn't appropriate on Facebook—will any of these photos come back to haunt these girls in the future?

> **TIP** Always be careful with what you put online, anywhere… photos, comments, thoughts, opinions. Don't write or upload something you might later regret!

While the terms we have mentioned will easily get you kicked out of Facebook, there are some unwritten rules you should be aware of.

They may not get you kicked out, but they could certainly lead to embarrassment or shame down the road.

Another example of a Facebook no-no is when Sandra Soroka decided to break up with her boyfriend via her Facebook Status update.[48] She felt her boyfriend was going to break up with her anyway so she would beat him to the punch and do it publicly. What followed was definitely not what she expected. Soon, the online community, through forums such as Digg.com, blog comments, Facebook messages, and more, criticized her for her public breakup; the resulting backlash caused her social Profiles and media to be removed.

While there are no set "rules" in this category, some tips that will help you stay safe, and avoid embarrassment and shame, are:

- *Only post pictures, comments, updates, etc. that your grandma would be proud of*—this might ensure you won't get hurt down the road when a boss or potential employer finds your profile. Remember, Facebook can always make your information even more public down the road—there is no telling what information you post will be accessible to others, even if they aren't your Facebook Friends.

TIP When responding to something posted on your Wall, click "Wall-to-Wall" to avoid posting back on your own Wall.

- *Be careful when talking about clients, coworkers, or employers*—in any conversation, consider that most things in Facebook get posted to your Friends' News Feed. There's nothing stopping one of your Friends from forwarding damaging information.

- *Avoid posting too much personal detail*—especially if you aren't that close with all of your Facebook Friends. It could be easy for one of them to find information such as "I'll be away next week on vacation," find out where you live, and rob you (or worse). No sense being paranoid, but it's always good to be safe when posting information anywhere online.

---

48. http://www.allfacebook.com/2007/12/dont-break-up-via-facebook.

- *Facebook Friends and interactions are real*—if it's something you would do in private in real life, do it in private on Facebook. One example of this is when Jesse accidentally exposed his brother's wedding announcement on his Facebook Wall. When you want things to be private, send them a private message, or even better, talk to them in person! Yes, "first life" does exist!

- *Don't incriminate yourself*—Keep in mind that everything you post on Facebook can be retrieved for use in court cases, law suits, criminal prosecution, and more. Don't post any documents that could be used against you later, even if you are innocent.

- *Add your children as Friends*—This is probably the biggest recommendation we could give to any parent. As parents (and older sibling), we know Facebook can be one of the best methods to know what your children/siblings/nieces/nephews are doing and where they are. It allows you to know who their Friends are, what Groups they associate with, and it gives you another method of communication that they are familiar with. Having your children as Friends on Facebook puts you on level ground with them and may even help you get to know each other better!

ACTION ITEMS

- Be careful! We're not sure if this is a legitimate "action item" but don't try and push your luck, especially when it comes to the Terms of Use!

- Review the Terms of Use. We're guessing most people don't read these legal documents but it might be worth thirty minutes to at least skim through it.

- If you have a list of thousands of people you want to invite as Friends, break the list down into several smaller lists and do it bit by bit over time.

- Resist the urge to upload racy photos, or enter dumb comments or off-color remarks on anyone's Profile, including your own, especially if you have any inclination to use Facebook to further your career or grow your business.

- If you get disciplined by Facebook, contact their customer support group at http://www.facebook.com/cs_forms/fshelp.php.

- Read the stories of Tom Swift and Harry Joiner on the links in the references.

QUOTES FROM FACEBOOK USERS

"My basic rule of thumb is don't post anything on-line anywhere, including Facebook, that you wouldn't want to share with your favorite grandmother. So don't post information about how you got drunk at a party or arrested after your college football team won a game or anything that an older person may disapprove of. Also, have a close look at your photos. Do they portray you in a mature, professional light? If they're goofy and funny, share them with your friends but don't share them through Facebook because your future employer may see them and not approve."

Steven Rothberg
http://www.collegerecruiter.com

"Take the time to coach your kids on the ramifications of what they post on-line. Employers and college admission directors can search some of the information on Facebook. What's "cool" to post on-line as a junior in high school could be what eliminates them from admission into a college a year later. Their profile picture of them partying or in a revealing pose might be what costs them a great internship or coveted position after graduation. Even younger Facebookers can be coached on user etiquette. Be alert to the fact that some kids may use Facebook as a form of "cyber-bullying" and remind your kids that Facebook is not the place to work out difficult issues with friends."

Barbara Safani
President
CareerSolvers.com

9 Additional Resources

There's no way a book like this is going to have all the answers for everyone. The purpose of this book is to help you understand how to use Facebook as a professional tool for your business or your career. There are many resources available to you that are either going to be more current and up-to-date (such as blogs) or meet a more specific need (such as books on how to develop Facebook Applications).

In this chapter we list some of the more popular resources. Remember that your favorite search engine might be the best resource for finding specific answers. All of these links are available on our website at:
http://www.facebookadvice.com.

Blogs, Articles and Videos

Official Facebook Blog—the official blog with news on releases, explanation of features, how things are being used, best practices, etc. It's not updated very frequently.
http://blog.facebook.com

Inside Facebook Blog—an excellent resource for information and commentary on Facebook including news, events, speculation, etc. http://www.insidefacebook.com)

All Facebook Blog—similar to Inside Facebook, this is another excellent resource. http://www.allfacebook.com)

Social Times Blog—by the writers of AllFacebook.com, less Facebook-oriented and more social network-oriented. http://www.socialtimes.com)

Stay N' Alive Blog—this is Jesse's blog and, while not always strictly social network-oriented, it has taken a social turn recently. A great source to get Jesse's opinion on social networking news and events. http://www.jessestay.com)

Social Optimize Blog—a blog written by Jesse's Social Consulting and Development company, SocialOptimize.com, and other contributors. The blog has a social network-oriented focus based on what's popular at the time. This is a great place to find research, news and other Facebook developments. http://www.socialoptimize.com/blog)

Facebook Application Reviews Blog—Rodney Rumford focuses his commentary and observations on Facebook Applications, giving terrific insight into what's new. He also blogs about other Applications issues including, of course, privacy as it relates to Beacon as well as other core Facebook design issues. http://www.facereviews.com)

How to Use Facebook Videos—Melissa Schenk has 15 useful videos showing you how to navigate around Facebook and use many of its features. From adding Notes and pictures to using your Wall to understanding Applications, the Home Page and connections, these are great videos. http://www.expertvillage.com/interviews/facebook-use.htm

How to Use Facebook without Losing Your Job Over It—Eric at Internet Duct Tape has an excellent post that walks you through various aspects of Facebook, mostly focusing on things to do to ensure

your privacy settings are appropriate. Considering the title of the post, our favorite section is called: "Don't Use Facebook at Work." We agree that if you don't want to lose your job over Facebook, one of the things to *not* do is use it at work!
http://tinyurl.com/2v7sep

Facebook Applications and Privacy—How to Configure Facebook Applications—another excellent post with pictures and descriptions on what you can do to optimize your experience with Applications, as well as ensure your privacy is set up in a way that works best for you.
http://tinyurl.com/2s63gk

Danah is confused by Facebook's Fans—Robert Scoble responds to various questions by Danah Boyd giving pretty good insight into some strengths and weaknesses of Facebook. With about 30 comments, each drilling down a little more on a particular topic, this makes for a terrific read.
http://tinyurl.com/2r2ktr

13 Reasons your Facebook Account will be Disabled—Facebook provides fun and games, and potentially business income, but there *are* boundaries. Thor Muller has an excellent post that explains 13 reasons Facebook might disable your account, even telling why Guy Kawasaki allegedly got his account disabled. Make sure to read the 30+ comments.
http://tinyurl.com/232c5p

Facebook Bans Recruiter—Harry Joiner used the system with just the tools he had within Facebook, but was subsequently banned. Even though he didn't do anything malicious or contrary to Facebook's written policy, he was still banned. This story-bordering-on-saga is a great example to help ensure that you understand the issues surrounding Facebook's ability to disable your account.
http://tinyurl.com/2hz92m

Mari Smith's Facebook Resources—Mari has three excellent resources, including online classes (http://www.facebookfortunes.com), audio of interviews (http://www.facebookinterviews.com), and an excellent user-friendly-non-geek blog (http://www.whyfacebook.com).

Should Businesses ban Facebook?—Krishna De has a thoughtful blog post regarding the issue of getting access to Facebook while at work, and how this impacts company and employee branding. http://tinyurl.com/36zpj4

Recommended Books

The Savvy Gal's Guide to Online Networking (Or What Would Jane Austen Do?)[49]—even though it says it's for "savvy gals," this book is for anyone that wants to get a grip on networking online. Written in a fun Jane Austen style (we've never read Jane Austen), this book has information for the beginner and the expert alike.

Marketing to the Social Web: How Digital Customer Communities Build Your Business[50]—Specifically written for marketers, this book answers questions that most business people have regarding how to use tools such as Facebook for marketing purposes.

I'm on LinkedIn—Now What???[51]—This is the other social networking book that Jason wrote. It will assist you in getting the most out of LinkedIn. Perhaps you could use both of these books to come up with a complete social networking strategy.

There are a few other books about using Facebook available on Amazon, but they didn't get stellar reviews. Critics commented that there was poor editing and the books were weak on the actual content and utility. You can find them by searching "Facebook" on Amazon, but make sure to check out the comments and ratings before you move forward.

Also, there are a number of books that are scheduled to be available in the Spring and Summer of 2008, including *Facebook Application Development*, *The Facebook Book*, and *Facebook for Dummies*.

If you are looking for help with developing a Facebook Application you can search for "Facebook developer" and find thousands of companies

---

49. http://savvygal.typepad.com.
50. http://www.marketingtothesocialweb.com.
51. http://imonlinkedinnowwhat.com.

willing to help. You might want to consider checking out some Applications that you like, or that seem to be making good progress. Find out who created the Application and contact them for a bid.

ACTION ITEMS

- Visit each of these blogs and look for at least one post that will help you develop or execute your Facebook strategy.

- Read at least one networking book (even if it's a classic).

- Visit our site at http://www.FacebookAdvice.com and sign up to receive posts in your e-mail.

- Send us your favorite Facebook or social networking resources via our site!

QUOTE FROM A FACEBOOK USER

"If LinkedIn is about no-nonsense business information and networking to communicate your strengths and your value, Facebook is a way to inject more of your personality into your brand while also communicating other on-brand messages. Make sure you have strong brand clarity as a guide for making many of the choices that Facebook and Facebook friends will present to you."

Walter Akana
Life Strategist and Owner
www.Threshold-Consulting.com

10 Conclusion

Is the Facebook hype justified? Or will this be another social network that has a lot of buzz around it and very little substance for career or business-minded professionals? Will there be other social networks that take its place, or will Google's Open Social steal the thunder as more social networks are empowered with widgetry and gadgetry, leaving Facebook in the dust?

We think the hype is justified—now and for well out into the future. But let's say this window of opportunity is going to last for only a year or two (it will last a lot longer, we think). Here are some reasons why you should still take advantage of it:

1. **One or two years is still very significant.** Where is your career, or your business, or your personal brand going to be in one or two years? You can either sit back and watch, or read as the skeptics write about whether Facebook has arrived or not, or wonder if it's worth it. Sitting back is not going to do much for your business or personal brand.

2. **"Everyone else is doing it."** Okay, this justification doesn't pass muster with the moms out there, but consider who is using Facebook now. It's not just the college kids,

and it's not just people posting about their latest and greatest party. There are professionals who are hiring managers, venture capitalist and angel investors, and people in purchasing capacities. Your audience is on Facebook—having a profile can ensure that they get the information they need about you (and/or your company) at their convenience.

3. **Businesses are doing it, too.** Maybe no one in your industry has yet developed a presence on Facebook, so why don't you be the first one there and do it right? You may have a first-movers advantage to create the first Group, or the first Application, and gain leading recognition. Work aggressively to create your community on Facebook or watch as your competition does.

4. **Real relationships are being found and nurtured on Facebook.** Since we started using Facebook our networks have expanded in a way that they otherwise wouldn't have. They are more diverse, including more people that are technologically hip and aware. It's important to grow your network, and Facebook provides a rich environment where we can do that.

5. **It really doesn't take that much time.** Review *Chapter 6, Your Facebook Strategy*, and you'll see that what is needed to have a meaningful presence on Facebook is probably going to take less time than you spent ordering and reading this book. Of course, there are things to do over time to maintain your presence, but by then you'll probably have your own system that allows you to get genuine value from Facebook.

6. **Let's say that it does "go away," and that something better takes its place.** You will be ready to optimize the "next best thing," having used Facebook as a testing ground, a place to learn and develop a strategy. When the next-best-thing comes along, you'll be prepared to determine the value it may provide you and take advantage of it, instead of wondering if it is going to be worth the effort.

By now you should feel you are prepared with the information you need to go forward with a solid strategy. Good luck!

ACTION ITEMS

- Go to http://www.facebookadvice.com and subscribe via RSS or e-mail to keep up on current Facebook information.

- Check out the links section of http://www.facebookadvice.com for hyperlinks to everything that is in this book.

- Add yourself as a fan to the "I'm On Facebook—Now What???" Facebook Page at http://www.facebook.com/profile.php?id=6816644117.

- Get started!

QUOTE FROM A FACEBOOK USER

"Many professionals in their 40's and 50's tend to shy away from Facebook and other online social tools. They assume they are for the younger crowd. But these online applications are not going away. It is in your best interest to have a presence and a working knowledge of how and why Facebook (and others) operates. You want to make sure that you can be found by those with opportunities, because this is where they live."

Thom Singer
Author/Speaker
http://www.thomsinger.com

Afterword

Facebook is the leading social network, but it goes beyond that. To me it is the replacement for the rolodex. Home of my new business contacts. Contacts that come with benefits. After all, those old business cards in your rolodex? They don't show you what applications that person has installed. Nor can you see what music they love, what sports they follow, or who their friends are.

Jason and Jesse have done a great job of digging behind the covers of Facebook. Facebook is one of those services that might seem pretty simplistic when you first use it, but there's a *lot* going on at this website. For instance, I've found that most people really haven't thought through the implications of the privacy features. You can make things pretty public, or very private to just your friends, but only if you tweak the settings.

More disturbingly, Facebook has a lot of control over whether you may continue to be a member or not. My account was recently "erased" for a day because I ran a script that wasn't allowed according to Facebook's Terms of Use. Did I get a warning? No. They turned off my account. And when I say "turned off" I mean *removed everything about me*. So, you should definitely pay attention to the chapter with rules and etiquette (*Chapter 7, Facebook for Business(es)*), lest you get kicked out. My account was added back within a few hours, but partly because I'm a popular blogger. I have gotten notes from people who still haven't been able to convince Facebook to add back their accounts.

This is a lot of power to give to one company that has so much of our digital lives within its walled garden. Look, I store my photos, my videos, and all my friends' info inside Facebook, and conduct business through its messaging, wall, forum, and other features.

On the other hand, I've gotten access to a lot of people I wouldn't have had access to otherwise, and I've kept up with my Friends' happenings in ways that I wouldn't have imagined before.

I get my news in new ways, too, thanks to a Facebook Application called Feedheads, which shows me news collected by thousands of other Facebook users. And that's only one of dozens of apps I have on my Facebook account, with many more to come.

Anyway, hope you enjoyed the book and can't wait to see you on Facebook. Unfortunately, Facebook currently has a limit of 5,000 friends and I'm at that limit, so I can't add more friends for the time being. Either way, I'd love to hear about your experiences with Facebook.

Robert Scoble
Social Media Expert, Blogger, Author
http://scobleizer.com/

About the Authors

Jason Alba

Jason is *the* career management evangelist. After getting laid off in January 2006, having great credentials and in a job-seeker's market, Jason could hardly get a job interview. He decided to step back and figure out the job search process and understand all of the available resources. Within a few months he designed JibberJobber.com, which helps professionals manage career and job search activities the same way a salesman manages prospects and customer data. Read Jason's award-winning blog at JibberJobber.com/blog, and his first book, *'I'm on LinkedIn -- Now What???'*

Jesse Stay

Jesse Stay is *the* Social Media Guru. A programmer since age 10, and having entrepreneurial skills that appeared early on—from setting up lemonade stands as a child, to having his own lawn mowing business as a teenager, to selling T-shirts, candy and snacks to his peers in high school, Jesse decided to combine these skills by developing Applications on Facebook when the Facebook Developer Platform launched.

One of his applications, from his "Holy Rolls" (www.holyrolls.com) Network of religious applications, on Facebook sold within two months to an undisclosed organization, and Jesse quickly realized the value of Facebook. He is now a Founding Partner in his own social media consulting and development agency, SocialOptimize.com, helping his clients develop their Applications to become some of the top Applications on Facebook. Jesse's clients range from those in the Fortune 500 to very small start-ups, showing that businesses, from large to small, can benefit by having a presence on Facebook.

Jesse fully recognizes the power that social media can bring to any organization and now consults with, and writes software for, platforms such as Facebook, Bebo, OpenSocial, Twitter, and many others. You can follow Jesse's activities on his Technology Blog "Stay N' Alive" at jessestay.com, or on his Social Media Blog at socialoptimize.com/blog.

Other Happy About® Books

Purchase these books at Happy About http://happyabout.info or at other online and physical bookstores.

I'M ON
LinkedIn
Now What???

JASON ALBA
Foreword by Bob Burg

HappyAbout.info

*Networking Online—
Making LinkedIn
Work for you!*

This book explains the benefits of using LinkedIn and recommends best practices so that you can get the most out of it.

Paperback: $19.95
eBook: $11.95

Internet your Way
to a New Job

THE HAPPY ABOUT GUIDE TO ONLINE JOB SEARCHING

By Alison Doyle

Find Your New Job!

Just a few years ago, you could upload your resume to one of the top jobs sites, click a few times to apply and consider your job search well underway. Today, that isn't enough. Learn what you need to know to build your career and find a new job.

Paperback:$19.95
eBook: $11.95

Gain perspective and plan for success!

This book provides knowledge and insight into the dynamics of technology, and shows the impact of changes brought about by the social Web.

Paperback:$21.95
eBook: $14.95

Learn How to Collaborate with Web 2.0 tools !

With the advent of Web 2.0, we are seeing dramatic changes in the way people interact with each other via the Internet. Blogs, Wikis, online communities, social networks, and distributed teams are just some of the ways these technologies are shaping our interactions.

Paperback: $29.95
eBook: $19.95

Praise for I'm on Facebook—Now What???

"I'm On Facebook - Now What? is an essential resource for Facebook users who want to experience the full potential of social networking, and get the most out of the opportunities most of us never knew were there. From getting started to gathering friends to building business, this book gives you the whole picture in a concise and interesting read."
Cary Snowden, VP, Product Management and Marketing
http://linkinguniverse.com

"As a working professional in the media/entertainment industry where connections and contacts are the name of the game, Facebook is quickly becoming the standard reference for building and developing relationships. 'I'm on Facebook- Now What???' is an invaluable way to understand and navigate the exciting, constantly expanding dynamic environment. My hats off to Alba and Stay for a book that has helped me on my travels through the world of Facebook."
Bill Sobel, Chief Connections Officer, NY:MIEG/The New York: Media Information Exchange Group,
http://www.nymieg.org

"I enjoyed every word of the book. Jason and Jesse took me on a journey to one of the hottest online spots in the world. They provided me with insight, a lot of answers and even some new ideas. Everthing you need to know about Facebook is there, and then some... I highly recommend that you grab a copy and that you read it today."
Jens P. Berget, http://slymarketing.com

"I learned more about Facebook in fifteen minutes from this book than I have in the entire year I've been using it. I learned not only what I can do and how to do it, but what should I be doing to help myself and my business. 'I'm on Facebook -- Now What ???' is the indispensable guide to professionals and business owners using, or considering using, Facebook."
Ted Demopoulos, Author, Effective Internet Presence

"Very easy to read! I didn't have a Facebook account and after reading this book, I now do! I'm convinced Facebook is worth my time. I do appreciate that Jason and Jesse are upfront in saying Facebook will be a tool some will want to use and others won't. I also appreciated learning the benefits and drawbacks of Facebook along with tips on how to use this networking link before joining. I'd highly recommend this book to anyone involved in or who is considering joining Facebook."
Terri Ferrara, Summit View Career Coaching,
http://summitviewcareercoaching.com

"'I'm on Facebook--Now What???' provides a complete guide to the popular social networking site. There's something for everyone in this book! Business or social, novice or pro, you'll find great tips to get the most out of Facebook."
Andrew Flusche, Attorney & Blogger,
http://legalandrew.com

"Who should read this book and why? Mom's and Dad's first and foremost, because if you have a teenager in high school or college, your teenager is probably on Facebook. Managers and leaders of organizations should read this book. You definitely have employees out there. And students need to read the book. It will help them make informed decisions about information they want to share with the world."
Darlene McDaniel, Interview Guru, Blogger,
http://www.interviewchatter.com

"As an efficiency consultant working with entrepreneurs, I encourage my clients to use new media in a smart and professional way. Jesse and Jason do a great job of covering every corner of Facebook, taking a newcomer from A-Z with plenty of useful tidbits for veteran Facebook users along the way. Much of the advice is applicable to other social networks, as well. Highly recommended reading for anyone who is planning (or re-thinking) their social media strategy!"
Marina Martin, Owner, TypeAs, Inc.,
http://www.TypeAs.com

Printed in the United States
126710LV00003B/160-171/P

9 781600 050954